DISCIPLE STORY

Every Christian's Journey

DISCIPLE STORY

GREGORY M. CORRIGAN

AVE MARIA PRESS Notre Dame, IN 46556

Rev. Gregory Corrigan is associate pastor of Holy Rosary Church in Claymont, Delaware. Although *Disciple Story* is his first book, he is a regular contributor to *Celebration, A Creative Worship Service.* Father Corrigan is a graduate of St. Meinrad College and holds his Master of Divinity degree from its School of Theology.

Scripture selections, unless otherwise noted, are taken from the **New American Bible with Revised New Testament**, copyright © 1986, by the Confraternity of Christian Doctrine, Washington, D.C., are used with permission. All rights reserved. No part of the New American Bible With Revised New Testament may be reproduced in any form without permission in writing from the copyright owner.

The story, "Ring-Worm Boy," by W. Dow Edgerton, from THEOLOGY TODAY, copyright © 1988 by W. Dow Edgerton. All rights reserved.

Excerpts from ZORBA THE GREEK, by Nikos Kazantzakis. Copyright © 1953, 1981 by Nikos Kazantzakis. Reprinted by permission of Simon & Schuster, Inc., New York. All rights reserved.

Excerpts from MERIDIAN, by Alice Walker. Copyright © 1976, by Alice Walker. New York: Pocket Books, Simon & Schuster, New York. All rights reserved.

Excerpts from PILGRIM AT TINKER CREEK, by Annie Dillard. Copyright © 1974 by Annie Dillard. Reprinted by permission of Harper & Row, San Francisco. All rights reserved.

Excerpt from "Both Sides Now," sung by Judy Collins, words by Joni Mitchell. Copyright by Joni Mitchell. Elektra Records. All rights reserved.

International Standard Book Number: 0-87793-408-8

Library of Congress Catalog Card Number: 89-84737

Cover and text design by Thomas W. Ringenberg.

Printed and bound in the United States of America.

By virtue of the creation
 and still more of the Incarnation,
  nothing here below is profane
for those who know how to see.
                        Teilhard de Chardin

This book is gratefully dedicated
to my teachers, especially
to my parents, Greg and Eileen
for teaching me
to love the telling of stories,
to B. Brandon Scott
for teaching me
to open my life to the word of God,
and to Gavin Barnes, o.s.b.
for teaching me
so much about hearing
and proclaiming the word of God.

ACKNOWLEDGMENTS

Three of the disciple stories in this book, "Gold," "Co-Disciples for the Kingdom" and "To Dwell in a House of Parables," were originally published in *Celebration*.

The list of disciples whom I wish to acknowledge is significant. My thanks . . .

to Douglas Martis, a fellow student and writer, who encourages me by his love and dedication to the word of God

to Janet Andrelczyk for her creative influence and support

to Therese and Tom Forsthoefel for their blessed friendship

to Francis Kenney who evens out the rough edges in my life by allowing me to hear God's laughter

to Bill Freburger, my editor at *Celebration*, who initially encouraged me and has provided helpful direction along the way

to Frank Cunningham and Ken Peters at Ave Maria Press for all their help

and to the holy people of Holy Rosary Parish, Claymont, Delaware, for having ears to hear.

CONTENTS

INTRODUCTION

Jesus said to those who believed in him, "If you continue in my word, you are truly my disciples" (Jn 8:31 *RSV*).

Each of the disciples who originally followed Jesus—the apostles, the women, the misfits, the outcasts—had a deeply personal yet unique relationship with him. For some it resulted from how they reacted to him; for others it was the profundity of the experience, the places where they met, or the quality of time spent with him. Peter, for example, by virtue of his longevity as a Messiah follower, surely must have had a different bonding to the Lord than, say, Nicodemus or the official at Capernaum, whose interaction with Jesus seems to have been minimal.

On the other hand, we can assume that certain brief encounters with Jesus, such as those of the woman with the hemorrhage or Zacchaeus, were of such significance and depth that they became the occasion of a permanent and powerful bonding to the Lord.

The point is, each disciple knew the Lord and traveled with him in his or her own unique way. As part of the travel experience, they each stopped along the road, they prayed, slept, ate, drank and worked, and did so many of the things people do in the course of day-to-day living.

The experience of the disciple with Jesus in the first-century Mediterranean world is similar to our own experience with Jesus: Both involve journeys and both reveal that we come to know him through many personal encounters. Like the original disciples, we too are asked to invest ourselves in a journey that requires real participation and commitment. We must continue in his word in all its fullness if we are to truly be called "disciples." To ensure our participation, it is important that we become part of the story.

The original disciples had the advantage of knowing Jesus himself or knowing people who knew him. Unlike us, however, they did not have the advantage of owning their own bibles so they could read the stories in the New Testament and see their effects. Story offers us perspective and reflection, an opportunity to participate in a variety of encounters with Jesus and let them change our lives. The Jesus stories are not something simply to be "read," however. We take the written word for granted because it is so accessible to us. It is not enough to read the words mechanically and vicariously, like we would some gothic novel. The stories of the New Testament are meant to engage us in a relational way as disciples of a Messiah who personally calls us to follow.

I am convinced that the reading of any text should be purposeful and participational. Yet we generally read in the way we were taught—indiscriminately, the random progression of sentences and paragraphs carrying us along with little reaction. With a text as important and alive as scripture, however, we need to read in such a way that we fully involve ourselves.

Disciple Story does not need to be read from cover to cover (although I hope it's read in its entirety!). Read it a piece at a time and allow time for reflection, or questioning, or even dialogue. If a thought sparks some interest in a relevant scripture passage, go read more of the scripture and let it communicate with you. Meditate on the word of God. See *yourself* as part of the story. If you feel drawn to a story out of sequence, then by all means read and pray with that one. Each story and each disciple in the journey with Jesus has its own character and ability to influence.

B. Brandon Scott, in *The Word of God in Words*, seeks to show how language can reveal God. He does not pretend to tell the reader what the Bible means. Rather, he seeks to form better readers. Reading leads to hearing and hearing leads to proclamation. He compares the reader of a biblical text to the performer of a musical score. It is a useful analogy as we approach *Disciple Story*.

> A piano is an instrument of music—it is not the music. In this it corresponds to the speech faculty. In speaking or reading we are not aware of mechanical devices, but they are present.
>
> More to the point is the musical score. It too is not the music but an inert series of dots on crossed lines. It corresponds to a book. In the mind of the composer there was music, but it is not the score. A score is the potential for music. It gives directions, but it needs, even demands, someone to perform it.
>
> A performer engages in a creative interaction with the score. We say a musician performs a score. Reading is a performance, and the text is a score that provides clues and directions for that performance.

So, we seek a little music here. I am not so inflated to think that the "score" I have written will produce a symphony. But perhaps an instrumental piece or two will be heard from time to time along with your creative playing of the words—the sad cry of an oboe that embellishes a moment of a Jesus text; or the brief, piping pitch of a piccolo that brightens the pace in the disciple journey.

The stories of Jesus were originally told by a speaker and heard by a listener. They were not read. But even reading, done with the goal of participating in the story, can be effective. Part of my attempt here is to help you share more intimately in the experience of hearing the stories and of becoming part of them.

Today, we have no way of knowing whether Peter had a loud, bellowing voice or Paul a stuttering problem. But we do know that the hearing of the Jesus story was so real and so effective that it changed listeners into believers; it made the dead come to life. We know that the proclamation of the Jesus story ushered in a kingdom of truth. The hearing of that Good News was the fulfillment of scripture.

We may deduce that the way in which Peter or Paul or any of the other women and men proclaimed the Jesus story was not in a literary, sentence by sentence, paragraph by paragraph style. Rather, their words were powerful because they were charged with the life of God. As we open this text, let us also open our ears and our hearts so that the same life of God may break into our world as we re-echo the disciple story.

Feast of the Immaculate Conception
Abbey of Gethsemani
Trappist, Kentucky

BEGINNING WORDS

> The eleven disciples made their way to Galilee,
> to the mountain to which Jesus had summoned
> them. At the sight of him, those who had enter-
> tained doubts fell down in homage. Jesus came
> forward and addressed them in these words:
> "Full authority has been given me
> both in heaven and on earth;
> go, therefore
> and make disciples of all the nations"
> (Mt 28:16-18 Lectionary version.)

I wonder how many fell down in homage at the sight of him. The text says they worshiped, but they also entertained doubts.

If I had been there I would surely have fallen down.

I have surely entertained doubts.

What is discipleship? What does it mean to be called? We picture the eleven faithful ones there on that mountain. Important things always happened on mountains. Moses received the commandments on a mountain. It was on the holy mountain that the whole people of Israel were called to worship the Lord God. And Matthew tells us that Jesus preached his famous sermon on a mountain.

Something special was in store for those eleven disciples that day when the resurrected Jesus, with full authority, commissioned them to go and make disciples of all nations.

It is a story that has been proclaimed, heard and shared for many centuries. It has come into our own time and for many of us, it has entered our ears and our hearts to become our own story, our way of living, our way of sharing with others.

So let us begin. Let us share something of the Life and the Truth that has been given to us. Let us share the Disciple Story.

DISCIPLESHIP

The 1985 Broadway musical *Big River* tells Mark Twain's story of Huckleberry Finn. Through action, song and dance we experience a portrayal of Huck Finn, the mischievous and misunderstood boy who questioned authority, disregarded the customs of his day, and had the courage to do what was "right" even though it meant his rejection by society.

In the opening song, the prudish Widow Douglas badgers Huck,

> "You've got to read your Bible
> if you want to go to heaven!
> If you don't
> go to hell!"

Huck doesn't know what to do. The bible-pounding adults in his life tell him that his salvation lies in reading the Bible and living like them. But he sees how they live:

—priggish, snobby and standoffish folks who care more about table etiquette than sharing food at table;

—busybody folks who can justify their gossipy tongues as long as they begin a meal by "praying grace";

—judgmental folks who pedestal themselves because they are Southern white or "proper," while making slaves of others because they are Black folks or "niggers."

Huck initially wants to go to heaven but figures, if heaven is full of people like the Widow Douglas and her sister Miss Watson, then maybe he'd have an awful time there.

Huck decides to go off on his own to find out for himself what life is all about.

On his rafting adventure down the Mississippi, Huck befriends the runaway slave, Jim. Huck sees in Jim the same good, human qualities that he has seen in people like himself—white people—and it makes him wonder how this can be. The turning point for Huck comes when Jim is captured and Huck must decide between doing the "decent and proper" thing—leaving Jim in slavery, or doing the worst possible thing, the thing that will, "no doubt, send me to hell!"—freeing him!

Huck chooses to free Jim and then marvels at "How good it feels to do the wrong thing."

The starting point in our consideration of discipleship is story . . . the Jesus story. If we are to break ground at all in terms of what discipleship means, who is called, how disciples are called, and what that discipleship means, we must first turn to the Jesus story.

The best source of information for the Jesus story is the Bible, of course. Unfortunately, today the Bible is greatly misused and abused—and underused. People are lazy. Many would rather sit in front of a television show that mocks or glamorizes life, instead of getting on a raft and riding the exciting adventure that living offers.

Ironically, it's the TV sitters who often bemoan their sad state of affairs and question why life is so dreary and meaningless.

"Lifers," people who really invest themselves in choosing life, may know excruciating pain at one point and exhilarating joy at another, but they are never bored or numbed. They are part of the goodness of life every day.

One of the advantages of exploring the Bible is that we can feel the grace-filled mist of the mighty river as it sprays off the bow in its winding journey through story. The life-stories of the Bible connect us with a history, a tradition, an experience of people and God. The stories touch us. They reveal something personal about our own story; they are part of the life we live today.

My father is a wonderful storyteller, and I used to love it when adults gathered at our house for some special day. Inevitably, they would tell stories and I would listen intently to the words that sparkled as they came from my father's mouth. Like a child moving in close to see the new baby, I would focus in on life as I heard the stories...

of my father's childhood

—doing without during the depression;

of my uncle's showmanship

—the minstrel at the neighboring church;

of my grandmother's five-ringed hand

—a child would show disrespect only once!

I would become part of that world. As I listened, the stories would stretch to include me, so that when I

had to do without,

or

found myself afraid to use my talents,

or

rebelled against the discipline my life needed,

I had a common point of reference, of understanding and affirmation that gave me the security and strength to go on.

The stories Mark Twain wrote about Huck Finn have a universal appeal because they contain the human values and range the human emotions that most of us experienced as adolescents. The details differ from person to person but we have all felt some pain of rejection, we have all had to struggle over what is the right thing to do.

The stories my father told are still alive, and the stories that I—and you—tell can be as well. More importantly, the stories which unfold from the Bible have broken open and re-membered the life of the person Jesus in households, shacks, churches and communities, through art, customs, liturgies and cultures, over a period of 2,000 years. Their power has not waned. Rather, their significance and meaning are renewed each time new ears hear them, each time new lips proclaim them.

The New Testament is chock full of stories; stories that vary from author to author, from character to character, from community to community. They all revolve around Jesus the Christ—"the God who fell from heaven," in John Shea's term. We will explore some of the Jesus stories that address the topic at hand—discipleship. We will attempt to retrieve some of their original intention. To do this we must respect story and try to hear what it says today. We must believe in the power of stories to effect in us some change or movement as disciples. We must respect the culture in which they were written, the language in which they were spoken, the people who have brought them to us.

Respecting story does not mean that we exalt it to a place beyond our reach. Too often, if people are bored by scripture, it's because teachers and preachers and religious types have floated scripture away on pious, drifting incense words. Jesus had a profound effect on his disciples because his words and stories were real; the disciples believed, and the stories became flesh.

To hear something of the creativity in scripture stories we must be willing to be creative—to look at the stories fresh, to hear them in a new way.

Why are these details here?
What might the disciples have thought when
that happened?
How does the story sound if I consider myself
a disciple?
What stories most affect my being a disciple?
Which do I refuse to hear?
How can I be a better disciple?
How do the stories of the world today speak
of discipleship?
How do my stories speak of discipleship?

In this book I will take some scripture stories about discipleship that have been handed down and share how I have heard them. My hearing of them is unique. It has been influenced by my education, my culture, my background and my prayer. My hearing of the Jesus stories is no better or no worse than anyone else's . . . just unique. The key is to hear them in their richness and truth, to allow them to touch the truth within us and to let our richness and goodness become part of the stories.

The stories we tell are by no means the only stories. There are many other scripture stories about discipleship and there are many disciple stories outside of scripture—those of the countless throngs of disciples who have lived and prayed in the past, those who witness today, and those to come—all are part of the discipleship that is commissioned by Jesus.

This book is a beginning. Disciples are people commissioned by their baptism to be followers of Christ—people meant to share their experience of Jesus, their stories of life, with others. The stories are not always fun. The people in them are not perfect. And ears are not always receptive. Huckleberry Finn discovered in his story that the Big River is often treacherous. But he said the words, he lived the adventure, and only then was he able to *be* the story.

Disciples know that the waters of baptism can be turbulent; following Christ can be demanding; the words of life often mean death. Yet, like those early disciples standing high on that mountain commissioned by the one with full authority who promises to be with them always, we have been raised up to be followers—we have been pedestaled! We stand out because of what we believe. We sink at times but are pulled back up by a man who fishes folks; we gasp for air and try once again to walk on water. Our success in life is often failure in the world's eye, and the greatest among us does not count for anything.

But the Rabbi who doodles in dirt is patient with us when we're anxious. The housekeeper God sweeps away our blindness and we see the lost silver coin. The celebrity Savior looks up at our modest sycamore house and says, "That is where I will dine!"

It is the Jesus story that makes credible our very life, and because of what he has done, we will live beyond our death.

Let us share the story of Good News.

Who Do You Say That I Am?

When Jesus went into the region of Caesarea Philippi, he asked his disciples, "Who do people say that the Son of Man is?" They replied,

"Some say John the Baptist, others Elijah, still
others Jeremiah or one of the prophets." He said
to them, "But who do you say that I am?"
(Mt 16:13-15).

Typically, one way that this gospel passage can be
prayed is to take that question as if Jesus were asking it of
us. And that makes a lot of sense. As disciples, we should
be able to make a confession of Jesus as Messiah. In an
even more personal way, we should be able to nuance our
confession according to what Jesus has done in our life—as
a friend, a lover, a companion, a challenge. But that's not
the only way to pray the passage.

One of the best ways to follow Jesus is to look at what
he did, the way he lived his life, and imitate him. Since Jesus asked others, "Who do you say that I am?", what
would happen if we asked other people, "Who do you say *I*
am?" Not who Jesus is . . . but *me*, who do you say I am?

I think it's a question worth asking. Too often the pri-
mary indicator of who we are, or who we think we are, lies
in opinions that we've formed about ourselves. Looking at
it either way, that opinion is biased. Some people are too
critical of themselves, too unforgiving, too demanding.
Other people are too easy on themselves, rationalizing
why they don't do better, making excuses for their faults
and bad habits. So, for a change, I pondered the question,
"Who do you say I am? . . . What can you say about me?"
and I thought about how people might respond if I asked
them.

Well, right off the bat, I thought that some would answer, "You're a priest." "You're a good person." "You're
prayerful." "You're holy." "You're funny!"

But I could also imagine others saying, "You're a
show-off." "You're arrogant." "You're a big mouth!"

So I think about specific individuals and how they might respond. I can think of some teenagers who would say, "You're pretty cool." But I have two nieces who would say, "You're pretty weird." I know an elderly woman who would say, "You're very kind." But there's an elderly man who would say, "You're very impatient." And I have a mother who would say, "You're wonderful!"

I finally gave up because I decided that I could probably think of as many different responses as there are people I know.

So I sat down and prayed quietly about it. What came to me was this: In the gospel passage when Jesus asks his disciples, "Who do you say I am?", who gives the right answer?—Peter. But even at that Jesus says to him, "You couldn't have figured it out on your own, Rock, and no other person could have given you the answer. Only the one who is in heaven could have revealed it; only God can answer the question." So the prayer becomes, "God, who do *you* say that I am?"

Go to your room, close the door and pray with that one for a while. The response is overwhelming. Oh, you may hear God whisper that you're still a little lukewarm and you've got to get more committed to what's going on . . . but, mostly, you're going to hear:

"You are loved. You are my very special child, a blessing to the world. You are beautiful and you are capable and I have made you my disciple, only once, just the way you are, because I know what goodness is. When you smile, my angels rejoice, and when you hurt, I cry. You are a gift, a present that I give to the world so that others can know how much I love."

At the end of the gospel story, Jesus strictly orders his disciples not to tell anyone the answer that God revealed about him. Ironically, in my prayer, God finished by saying:

"Too many of my children can't hear me or they refuse to hear me, so I want you to go and tell them who I say they are. Tell them what they mean to me. And then tell them to tell others."

And then God said,

"Amen."

Gold

He [Jesus] . . . came to his native place accompanied by his disciples. When the sabbath came he began to teach in the synagogue, and many who heard him were astonished. They said, "Where did this man get all this? What kind of wisdom has been given him! What mighty deeds are wrought by his hands! Is he not the carpenter, the son of Mary, a brother of James and Joses and Judas and Simon? Are not his sisters here with us?" And they took offense at him.

Jesus said to them, "A prophet is not without honor except in his native place and among his own kin and in his own house." So he was not able to perform any mighty deeds there, apart from curing a few sick people by laying his hands on them. He was amazed at their lack of faith. He went around to the villages in the vicinity teaching (Mk 6:1-7).

Alice Walker is a popular contemporary writer. A

young Black woman from the south, she grew up in extreme poverty and adversity, and much of the power in her writing is a direct result of her own experience. She has known much rejection.

The Christian journey has shown that rejection is a regular encounter for disciples. It's the undertow that sweeps against those who are committed to Christ. But even rejection, if understood through the story of Jesus, can be a witness, an example of how a disciple can persevere and even triumph despite opposition. It need not be ultimately destructive. Like precious metal that is refined by searing, intense heat, rejection can be a catalyst for virtue in the Christian disciple who has eyes to see and ears to hear.

One of Walker's novels, entitled *Meridian*, is a collection of stories about a young Black girl from the south. Though written in novel form, much of it is autobiographical—stories taken from Alice Walker's own experience.

One vignette in the novel is about gold. It tells about the heroine, Meridian, who one day discovers a large chunk of heavy metal. Meridian takes a large file and scrapes away the layers of rust that surround the metal. To her amazement, she finds that her possession is a bar of yellow gold.

Meridian rushes home to her mother who is sitting on the back porch shelling peas.

"I've found some gold!" she shouts.
"Gold!" and she places the large heavy gold bar on her mother's lap.

"Move that thing," her mother says sharply. "Don't you see I'm trying to get these peas ready for supper?"

"But it's gold," she insists. "Feel how

heavy it is. Look at how yellow it is. It's gold, and it could make us rich!"

But her mother was not impressed. Neither was her father or her family or her friends. Meridian has something wonderful to share but she is rejected. No one is interested in sharing her joy.

So Meridian took the bar of gold and put it in a shoe box and buried it under the Magnolia tree that grew in the yard. About once a week she dug it up to look at it. Then she dug it up less and less . . . until finally, she forgot to dig it up at all.

We have all experienced the pain of rejection. How awful it is when others don't believe in us or allow us to share with them the good things that we can offer. It is especially painful when the rejection comes from those whom we love the most: our family, our friends, those who know us.

Jesus certainly experienced this pain. In the passage from Mark's gospel, he had come back to his hometown to proclaim the Good News, to share his love, to heal and to minister to those whom he loved so much.

And he was rejected.

Ironically, he was rejected by those people because they knew him so well.

"We know this guy.

He's the carpenter, the son of Mary.

Who is he trying to fool?"

They put limits on who Jesus could be. They restricted him to their narrow understanding of who he was. They refused to see who he had really become. We all do it. It seems to be something inherent in human nature.

From my own experience, there are people who knew me when I was young, who, when told that I became a priest, are simply amazed.

"Not him, why he's the boy who used to steal tomatoes from our back yard!"

"Not that one, why, he was as ornery as they come!"

"How could he work for the church?!"

We all have a treasure to share with others. In fact, our life, our experience and our love improve only when shared with others. Our life is like that chunk of metal, rusty and in need of improvement. So we work at it. We file and scrape away the bad, the rust, and we find that we have something beautiful, something rich that shines before others, encouraging them to shine as well.

When we are rejected we have a tendency not to try at all, to let the treasure get buried within us. We know it's still there and occasionally a ray of its goodness may stream forth. But if we allow it to remain there, in time we'll forget all about it.

Jesus knew the pain of rejection. But he also knew how to handle it. He didn't bury what he had to share. He didn't give up. He simply moved on to others who would listen to him and receive the goodness, the treasure that he wanted to share.

I mentioned earlier that much of Alice Walker's writing is autobiographical. As an oppressed Black woman she has known much rejection. And she writes about it in her novels. From the story I shared it may sound like she doesn't deal too well with rejection. For in the story, Meridian gives up, she buries the gold bar and in time she forgets all about it.

But in reality, Alice Walker didn't give up. Despite rejections, she worked very hard to use her experience, to collect her stories and put them on paper so that she could share them with others. And countless thousands have been fitted with grace because of her. And, at a very young age, Alice Walker has been awarded a Pulitzer Prize in literature for her work.

When I really look at the people in my world I see much gold. Oh, there are some rusty layers that need to be filed away. Looking at me, people see that I myself have lots of filing to do. The key is to focus, not on the rust, but on the gold . . . not to reject, but to share our treasure with others and to encourage them to share with us.

Whatever goodness I've been able to share is because people have not rejected me. And because of that, it is easy for me to see others' goodness.

Gold!

We are the light of the world.

Let that light shine for all to see!

And Who Is My Neighbor?

There was a scholar of the law who stood up to to test him and said, "Teacher, what must I do to inherit eternal life?" Jesus said to him, "What is written in the law? How do you read it?" He said in reply, "You shall love the LORD, your God, with all your heart, with all your being, with all your strength, and with all your mind, and your neighbor as yourself." Jesus replied to him, "You have answered correctly. Do this and you will live." But because he wished to justify himself, he said to Jesus, "And who is my neighbor?" (Lk 10:25-29).

"Disciple" is one of those religious catchwords. Some people attach it to certain holy people of history—saints and martyrs. For others it is a sanctimonious term that doesn't mean anything. Some people associate it primarily with its use in the scripture stories. Most people tend to distance themselves from the word, to place it outside the personal, present reality in which they live.

Yet, disciples abound. And just as Jesus flip-flopped people's understanding of God's activity in the sacred and the profane, so our stories today have the same capacity for changing narrow vision. We must abandon the safe, familiar roadway and travel fresh down a new frontier. Although seemingly in danger, we are secure. There is a presence of goodness that guides our way. We are changed along the journey. When we reach a point of rest and the travel dust settles, we are given a clearer glimpse of our footing, our placement. We see for the first time and are able to recognize the most unlikely disciples. Surprisingly, when the lighting is just right, we are even able to see a "disciple" when we look in the mirror. It's all in a story.

A while back I happened to watch a show called *The People's Court.* You've probably seen it: People who have filed a suit in small claims court waive the right to have their case heard there and agree to present their case in this TV courtroom, and to abide by the decision of the television judge. It's one of those shows that ranks right up there with other great ones like *Gilligan's Island.*

On the show I saw, they presented "The Case of the Unfriendly Neighbor." A suit was brought by a middle-aged woman against her next door neighbor, a young man. The woman claimed that they had been "good neighbors" and had agreed to split the cost of a wall that was built between their properties. After the wall was completed, the young man refused to pay his half so the woman took him to court.

The young man agreed that they had been good neighbors and had agreed to splitting the cost of the wall. But, he argued, the wall was not built according to the original plans, was poorly built, and was on five inches of his property—not part of the agreement. In retaliation, he had filed a counter suit asking for damages so that he could build another wall next to the one already there.

As the show went on, the disagreement got more and more heated and I finally turned it off. I never found out the verdict because I got tired of watching these "good neighbors" yell at each other and call each other "liar."

So, who is my neighbor? Well, Jesus tells us. It's a story of the good Samaritan, one we've heard many times. And perhaps because we've heard it so often, or because the "good" Samaritan has become synonymous with some "nice person" or do-gooder, we fail to get the real impact of the story. We don't hear it the way people did when it was first told by Jesus.

Jesus did not tell this story to 20th-century Americans. To his first-century hearers many elements in the story would have meant something far different than they do to us today. "There was a man going down from Jerusalem to Jericho," for example, doesn't say much to us. But the original hearers knew that that road was extremely dangerous. Those who used it most were robbers and other criminals. Decent folks used an alternate route. So when Jesus said that the man fell in with robbers, the audience would not have been surprised. In fact, they probably would have thought, "If he was stupid enough to use that road, he deserves what he gets."

Another striking difference in the way we hear the story shows up in the appearance of the Samaritan. As mentioned before, when we hear "Samaritan" we think of a do-gooder. But first-century Palestinians hated Samaritans. When they heard the story, they probably thought, "The Samaritan is going to finish the job the robbers started."

Instead of explaining all the elements in how we hear scripture stories differently today, perhaps I can get the point across by re-telling the story using a modern scenario. (St. Luke forgive me!)

There was a white-robed member of the K.K.K. walking through Black Harlem in New York City about 11:30 on a Saturday night. The man was jumped by muggers who stripped him of his white robes, beat him and then went off leaving him half dead.

A priest happened along. He saw the man lying in the gutter, but because he had to get up early the next day for Sunday Mass he decided he couldn't help him. He did, however, tell the man, "I will pray for you."

Likewise, a young man driving through the area, a seminarian, saw the man lying in the gutter. He knew that the man was hurt and needed help but he thought to himself, "This case has not been referred to me by Catholic Social Services, so I better not get involved." And off he drove.

After a long time another man came driving along ... a Black man. The Black man saw the other man lying in the gutter and he was moved to pity at the sight. He approached him and bandaged some of his wounds. He then carried the man to his car and drove him to the hospital. The hospital required cash payment for emergency services so the Black man paid the bill. He then gave the cashier enough money to cover several days' stay at the hospital. He also told the cashier that he would be back in a few days and would pay whatever bills remained.

Sound far-fetched? Well, in a way, it is, but probably not any more than Jesus' story. To inherit everlasting life, Jesus says we must love our neighbor as ourself. That means breaking down the walls that exist between us and the people who live next door. But it also means more.

As disciples, we are called to break down the walls of prejudice and the barriers of indifference that exist between us and other people in the world.

And who is my neighbor?

The answer came,

The one who treated him with compassion.

"Then go and do the same."

What's in a Name?

As John watched Jesus walk by he said, "Behold, the Lamb of God." The two disciples heard what he said and followed Jesus. Jesus turned and said to them, "What are you looking for?" They said to him, "Rabbi" (which translated means Teacher) "where are you staying?" He said to them, "Come and you will see." So they went and saw where he was staying, and they stayed with him that day . . .

Andrew, the brother of Simon Peter, was one of the two who heard John and followed Jesus. He first found his own brother Simon and told him, "We have found the Messiah" (which is translated Anointed). Then he brought him to

Jesus. Jesus looked at him and said, "You are Simon, the son of John; you shall be called Kephas" (which is translated Peter) (Jn 1:35-42).

A fundamental mark of discipleship is being called by Jesus . . . called by name. The tradition is explicitly clear. The disciples are personally called by Jesus, who knows them, draws them to himself, then asks them to leave all behind and follow him.

Some are even asked to give up their previous names. All are asked to abandon previous identities.

My niece Brianna is five, and for the past year and a half she's been absorbed in that wonderful part of childhood known as "make believe." She has been known to tell the most unusual stories about the strangest things. But mainly her make believe has been about herself. We don't know where she picked it up (her older sister Andrea never did it), but she has gotten into the habit of changing her name.

It all started about a year ago. She decided that her new name would be "Amy." Then a few months later she became "Michelle." Her latest label is "Jessica Lynn." And the kid is serious about it! She refuses to answer to "Brianna." Her name is now Jessica Lynn!

Ironically, her mother, her grandmother and others play along, and they call her by the name she chooses. But I'm too smart for that. With all my psychology and sophistication, I'm not going to give in to this little kid, right?

I have tried to catch her off-guard, to get her to respond to her real name. I would creep into the room while she was watching television and I'd holler, "Brianna!" But she is clever. She'd turn quickly, and then just as quickly she'd say, "My name is Jessica Lynn."

After several attempts (and failures) at this, I grew understandably frustrated. That's when she turned the tables on me. She looked at me quite directly and said, "What do you want . . . George!" "George!" I screamed. "My name isn't George! Don't you try that goofy stuff with me." And in that incredible, know-it-all and very innocent way that only kids have, she said, "Are you mad at me, George?"

I was ready to sell the child into slavery, but her mother wouldn't let me.

I was reminded of this story when thinking about the above gospel passage. There's a lot in the gospel story that has to do with names. John says, "Look, there goes the Lamb of God," a name he has given to Jesus. One of the disciples calls Jesus Rabbi, a name which means, "Teacher." They call him Messiah, a name which means "Anointed." And, in the climax of the story, Jesus meets Andrew's brother Simon for the first time and he says to him, "Your name is Simon; your father's name is John; your name now shall be Kephas (but we'll call you Peter, Rocky!)."

I wonder how Peter felt. No "Hi," no "How do you do?" no "Pleased to meet you." Simply, "I'm changing your name. We'll call you 'Rocky'!"

This action of Jesus meant so much, especially in the religious experience of the Jews. To name something or someone meant that you had power over that thing or that person. In Genesis, God tells Adam to name all the beasts and animals, for he is to have dominion over them. In a contrasting way, humankind was not able to name God, for people could not have control over God. When Moses asked God, "What's your name?", God responded with a play on words, "I Am What I Am."

So now Jesus comes along looking for disciples, and in their first interaction he tells Simon that he is taking over, "You're with me. I'm in charge, I'm in control. You are my disciple—Peter." And ironically, Peter, like the other two disciples, follows. He senses something about this person Jesus that makes it clear that Jesus is right. Peter shows a great deal of humility.

We live in a world where we all want to be our own master; we want to determine what we will do and how and when we will do it. And ultimately, as long as we live that way, we'll be off track, unfulfilled, lacking in a significant way. To really have life, we must die. Disciples must relinquish control and trust that God will lead them in the way they are meant to travel.

Jesus is calling us by name. We must hear what we are being called: "Disciple," "Martyr," "Christian." We must accept our name and live all that that entails.

Let us pray for each other, for the grace to follow the Lord.

My only concern is: I have this fear that someday I'll die and I'll arrive at the gates of the kingdom, and Peter and all the angels and saints will come out to meet me and Peter will say, "Welcome! We've been waiting for you . . . George!"

WHO IS CALLED ?

The story of the people of Israel, the story of the people of Jesus, is the story of a God who calls. Scripture is full of this theme—someone being called. We learn something about the "God who calls" by looking at who is called. . .

God called Abraham
—an old man with an old pregnant wife, to lead the people. Whoever heard of such a thing? Today we don't even pay attention to old people.

God called David
—a boy who is described as having a "ruddy complexion." Is that what made him a good king?

God called Joseph
—a kid of the Old Testament who told people his dreams;
—an old man in the New Testament who listened to his dreams.

God called Mary
—a virgin teenager who was filled with God. She was specially chosen. (I've always had a feeling that teenagers were special!)

God called Peter
—a good-hearted but thick-headed fisher, whom Jesus

nicknamed "Rocky." Let's hear it for the regular folks! God called Paul
—a bitter widower who hated much. The light of Jesus blinded him so that he could see. Thank God for conversion.

The list goes on. What stands out when looking at the disciples whom God called is that they are all so very, very human. We see their heartaches and their headaches, their grey hairs, their bad teeth, their "yucky" complexion. We see their many mistakes, but we also see their many miracles. And in seeing how God trusts such ordinary folks with such extraordinary grace I come to believe that this God would call someone like you . . . someone even like me.

For whatever reason God fancies people like you and me. If you have a little quirk, if I seem a little weird, that's o.k. with God. And if you're really strange or I'm really different, God seems to pay attention even more. God goes out of the way for those who are different: the outcast, the neglected, the poor, the hurting. God seems to prefer those whom most people ignore or despise. God seeks out people who don't know where they are going. The God who makes disciples desires to be in relationship with each one of us, to share in a dynamic way an intimacy that is akin to the breath that is shared when lovers kiss. The God of Abraham, Isaac and Jacob wants to be the God of Abraham, Isaac, Jacob and *you* . . . and *me!* Each of us is special to God, as we are, and God will come to meet us wherever we are.

There's a wonderful love story at the end of John's gospel that has to do with the dense disciple Rocky, Simon Peter. My thanks to the intelligent theologians who helped me with this one because in order to really appreciate the story we have to know a little Greek.

In the Greek there are several verbs that can be used for "love." The two most often used are

agapas—the most intense love; that very unique relationship, like the love the Father shares with the Son,

and

philos—the kind of love that is shared by friends, buddies.

In the appendix to the gospel of John we hear Jesus asking Peter three times if Peter loves him. We all know the story. Peter finally gets frustrated because Jesus keeps at it. But maybe it was Jesus who should have gotten frustrated. Let's look at the story in the original Greek. Jesus said to Simon Peter,

"Simon, son of John, do you love me (*agapas*) more than these?"

He said to him, "Yes Lord; you know that I love you (*philos*)."

He said to him, "Feed my lambs."

A second time he said to him,

"Simon, son of John, do you love me (*agapas*)?"

He said to him, "Yes Lord; you know that I love you (*philos*)."

He said to him, "Tend my sheep."

He said to him the third time,

"Simon, son of John, do you love me (*philos*)?"

Peter was grieved because he said to him the third time,

"Do you love me (*philos*)?"

And he said to him,

"Lord, you know everything; you know that I love you (*philos*)."

Jesus said to him,

"Feed my sheep."

First, Jesus asks Peter if he loves him in that most incredible way (*agapas*). But Peter either doesn't hear it or he isn't able to meet Jesus at such a place. So he responds, "You know that I love you (*philos*; read: like a buddy)." So Jesus challenges him again, and Peter makes the same response. Finally, Jesus meets Peter at the place where Peter is stuck. He says, "Peter, do you love me (*philos*)?" And Peter responds, "Well, that's what I've been telling you! Of course I love you! (*philos*)."

Jesus was calling Peter to something very unique, very special. But Peter wasn't ready for it, or didn't understand it, or couldn't respond to it. Jesus didn't abandon him. Rather, Jesus met him at the level he understood. Jesus loved him where he was able to love.

One of the encouragements I take from this story is that God doesn't desert us; God loves us as we are able to love. We may be called to be or to do more, but if we can't hear or aren't able at this time, God will remain faithful. God's love is not conditional. God loves us anyway.

The Light of the World

Thus says the LORD:
"This, rather, is the fasting that I wish:
Sharing your bread with the hungry,
 sheltering the oppressed and the
  homeless;

Clothing the naked when you see them,
   and not turning your back on your
   own.
Then your light shall break forth like
   the dawn. . ." (Is 58: 6,7-8).

Jesus said to his disciples:
"You are the salt of the earth.
But what if salt loses its taste?. . .
It is no longer good for anything. . . .
You are the light of the world. . . .
So, your light must shine before others. . ."
(Mt 5:13-16).

Those who are called to discipleship are not being asked to join a fan club. Disciples are part of a personal communion, a unity that requires everything. Jesus was often called Rabbi—he certainly acts like a teacher; but most significantly, he is our Lord. He is the one who carried the cross, showing us what we must do. As a disciple-singer puts it, he is the one who

"endured the burning of the fires that purged
   the darkness into day
      giving Light
(He) took the fear out of dying;
   I'll walk straight
   through the burning with you
      giving Light" (J. Keith Zavelli).

Our self-awareness is grounded in his self-awareness, a consciousness that shines with the goodness of our wonderfully created beings. We are good by virtue of the fact that God has made us. That goodness, which has been so generously bestowed on us, must in turn be shared with others. Jesus continues to shape who we are as disciples, making us more authentic and more loving. We become more like him, and his goodness, refracted through us, becomes a bright promise for tomorrow's disciples.

I ran into a young friend the other day. I taught her "theology" in the eighth grade last year. (Kids today are too sophisticated to be taught "religion.")

Now she's all grown up in high school . . . a ninth grader! We talked for some time and she told me how things were going. She's a good girl and she works hard; she's been on the honor roll and she was even elected to the student council.

She also told me about a paper she had to write for her theology class—a paper on who they thought was a modern day prophet. She flattered me by telling me that she had considered writing her paper on me. Ultimately though she changed her mind because she decided I was too weird. I pointed out to her that John the Baptist was a prophet and he was pretty weird. "True," she conceded, "but Father, he wasn't as strange as you are!" (I may be weird but at least I don't eat grasshoppers!)

As we talked everything she said sounded positive. But I somehow sensed that something was bothering her. She finally admitted that she's been depressed because she's one of the few girls in her class who wasn't invited to the Valentine's Dance. She said it's because she's not as pretty as the other girls.

I told her I thought she was beautiful, and I meant it. She's bright and friendly and she always attracts people because of the way she makes each person feel important. But try as I might, I could not convince her. She kept on feeling bad for herself, failing to recognize how wonderful she is.

There's a terrible tendency in the world for people to focus on what they think they are, instead of giving thanks, and simply enjoying, what they are.

Jesus doesn't say to his disciples, "You *are going* to be the light of the world." He says, "You *are* the light of the world." We are not called by God to be anything other than what we are. And God has made us just the way God wants us to be. All this light, and still we find it so difficult to see.

Instead of recognizing and giving thanks for good healthy bodies, we find ourselves fretting about "my yucky hair" which never does what I want it to.

Instead of enjoying the creative, questioning mind that God gave us, we choose to sit rotting in front of a TV and then we wonder why life seems so drab.

Instead of beaming in the knowledge that we are Light, we complain because we're not a high-tech laser, or because we're only 25 watts instead of 60 watts. In so doing, we diminish ourselves, and others.

Instead of seeing that we are salt—rich and flavorful—able to season others with our goodness and experience, we rue the fact that we're not . . . pepper!

We're always wishing we were something else . . . somebody else.

What would happen if each one of us finally accepted what God made us to be? No more arguing about it, no more rationalization, just final acceptance and approval of how wonderfully we are made?

A couple weeks ago, I wrote this prayer:

A Praise Prayer

A summer in January
when the sun is so proud
of all that it is,

and it runs after you
and you can hardly see,
but you can feel it all over
(even in your ears!).
  This is the kind of surprise
  that is better
  than a man standing at your door
  with a UPS package.
This is the kind of day
that if you stay indoors
and refuse to go outside,
it's like giving the finger
to God.
Now I wish I was a centipede,
and I would take off all fifty pairs
of my white high-top all-star Converse,
and feel the clean earth
through my bug toes.
  And from the ground I wish I was a tree,
  stretching all of my branches and twigs
  up to the sky,
  trying to reach the sun
  that so easily reaches me.
And from the tree I wish I was a bird,
that could
acrobat without a net
between the dirt and the stars.
  And from the bird I wish I was a song,
  Music
  that sings praise
  to the Composer.
And then I realize . . .
I am.
  "My whole being proclaims
  the greatness of the Lord."

We are not called by God to be anything other than what we are.

We are the light of the world!

Looking Out For # 1

When Jesus saw the crowds, he went up on the mountain, and after he had sat down, his disciples came to him. He began to teach them (Mt 5:1).

Christian disciples have a remarkable propensity for missing the point (Aurelius Boberek).

From the earliest times, disciples have evidenced what can be called (rather bluntly) a lack of understanding. They have been challenged by outsiders, by the church, and by each other . . . and justifiably so. Disciples often just don't get it. They miss the mark and show their bungling, messy, authentically human side.

Fortunately, God doesn't expect perfect followers. God expects genuine people, people who may screw things up at one point, but who are then able to learn from their mistakes and do better the next time. Fortunately, too, Jesus is a teacher, a teacher who graciously takes the time to sit in our midst and teach us what we need to know about being disciples . . . even when we don't like it.

I hate it when I find out I'm wrong. A long time ago someone gave me a bumper sticker that read "God made the Irish # 1." I knew that, because I'm Irish. But I was proud to see it in writing and to realize that others knew it as well.

Then one day I'm driving along and I see this bumper sticker on the car ahead of me: "God made the Italians # 1." Can you imagine? I mean, they're pretty good with spaghetti, but number one? And to top it off, another time I'm walking to my car in a parking lot and I see a bumper sticker: "God made the Polish # 1."

Well that did it! I may be naive but I'm not stupid. I realized then that there's probably all kinds of these bumper stickers driving around—and they're all meaningless! Some Irish guy had them made up to pat the Irish on the back, and the Italians did the same to brag about themselves, and the same with the Polish, and the Germans, and the French, and everybody else. Everybody's just pretending that God made them number one.

It was more than a year ago that I found out who God really made # 1. It was February 24, and after a long time of thinking and worrying and praying, I decided to spend the night walking the streets of Philadelphia so I could give out sandwiches to homeless people. I don't know what made me do it but I knew I had to.

I announced my decision at dinner that night and the pastor, Father Forester, looked at me with that look, you know, the one that says, "Oh dear Jesus, what's he going to do now?"

The forecasters were calling for up to two inches of snow that night with low temperatures in the mid-teens. I bought some bread and some peanut butter, made up a knapsack full of sandwiches, dressed in many layers, called a few friends to tell them to pray for me (and what they should do with the body if I didn't survive!) and off I went to center city Philadelphia.

It wasn't hard to find the homeless—they were everywhere: On any corner where you saw steam rising from the grate you could bet there was a ragged, smelly resemblance of a person sprawled on top of it.

It wasn't hard to find other "creatures of the night" walking the streets either. And lest I give the impression of my having done something virtuous or heroic ... I didn't. I was scared to death. I ran a lot that night. And I hid a lot. And at times I even went back to sit in my car for a while because the cold was so very cold.

I was even afraid of the people sleeping on the pavement, those people in their cardboard beds. I would timidly go up to them and leave a sandwich by their hand. Then I'd back off. Sometimes, when they were awake and saw me coming close, they would back away because they were afraid of me. Only one homeless person spoke to me directly and that was to say "Thank you."

The night lasted much longer than my supply of sandwiches, and finally the sun began to rise; it was time to go. As I pulled out of the city, at 21st and Walnut, I saw a man sleeping on the corner and I knew I'd have to come back again.

> Blest are the poor.
> Blest are the lowly.
> Blest are those who are persecuted.

Throughout history our God has revealed to us a special love for the poor, a preference for those in society who are weak and powerless. They are blessed.

The story of Jesus is an offer of love which is extended to all people, but Jesus clearly takes the side of those who are in most need, physically and spiritually. This "preferential option for the poor" is not some accessory virtue. It is a requirement of our faith. As disciples, we are called to be defenders of the defenseless, workers for social justice, sharers in the bounty we have received. We are each required to ask ourselves some very serious questions:

How do I live?
Am I wasteful?
Do I eat too much while others go hungry?
What about the things I own?
How important to me are material possessions?
Have I helped someone?
Am I making a difference?

We are called to experience the power of God in the midst of poverty and powerlessness.

I hate it when I find out I'm wrong. I now know the truth. I now know who God made number one. And I know that I'm supposed to create a bumper sticker. I'm supposed to live in justice, in a way that shows every person as a child of God. Every person is entitled to be treated with respect and the sense of awe and wonder that rises in the presence of something sacred.

God made the Poor # 1.

The Prodigal

Then Jesus said, "A man had two sons, and the younger of them said to his father, 'Father, give me the share of your estate that should come to me.' So the father divided the property between them. After a few days, the younger son collected all his belongings and set off to a distant country where he squandered his inheritance on a life of dissipation" (Lk 15:11-13).

The movie "Harry and Son" stars Paul Newman and Robby Benson as a father and son who have a very rocky relationship. The father is a very serious type and he's upset because he's unemployed. The son is the happy-go-lucky type, unemployed, and not very serious in his attempts at getting a job. This infuriates the father, adding even greater strain to their relationship.

The movie shows a lot of their arguments and fighting, and yet we can see they love each other very much. In the end the son returns home to find that his father has died suddenly. The closing scene has the son sitting on the beach with his girlfriend, talking about his father: "I wanted him to have everything. I wanted him to have it all. I guess there just wasn't enough time."

We've all heard the story of the prodigal son many times, so there's a tendency not to take it too seriously. But it is a story that speaks to disciples. The range and uniqueness of the characters in this drama evidence the broadly diverse arrangement that God has so carefully orchestrated. It is a story that includes disciples we might not have chosen had we been in charge of casting. It is a story that sets up a challenge. We are made aware of how very much we have been given and, in light of God's example, we are to consider our own generosity and capability for forgiveness. It is a story that helps us to hear in new ways, a cotton swab that gently removes the hard wax of our hearts. If we really have ears to hear the Good News, it will change the world.

Classically, we're told that there are three ways to "hear" or become part of this story. By inclination, people have a tendency to put themselves in the place of the prodigal son. We've all done wrong. We know the incredible goodness that comes in changing our bad ways, repenting and doing good. Doing it in a very dramatic way like the prodigal son is something we've all probably dreamed about.

Many commentators today, however, want us to hear the story or become part of it by taking the place of the elder son. They say that, realistically, most of us go through life towing the line and doing what is expected, not doing anything too great, and not doing anything too awful, just standing on the outskirts, feeling somewhat jealous if someone else does well.

In tradition, the third character of the story, the father, represents God. And rightly so. In ways more like a mother, this God-figure with arms outstretched waits for the child's return: embracing, kissing, full of forgiveness and celebration for the one who was lost and now is found.

Perhaps a way to really hear the story is to place ourselves within each character

—to learn something from the obstinacy and envy of the elder son: to see the futility of standing on the outside, afraid to be part of the celebration of life;

—to learn from the prodigal son: to know the ultimate destructiveness of some of our ways and be willing to make a drastic change . . . before it's too late!

The younger son wallowed in the mud with the pigs, but he didn't wallow in guilt. He saw where his life needed changing and he acted on it right then.

How many of us are going to become saints . . . someday? Or really take advantage of the holy opportunities of our lives . . . someday? How many are going to wind up saying, "There just wasn't enough time." The time is now!

And then there's the father who acts like a mother, the one who represents God. Yes, we're supposed to put ourselves in God's place too—maybe more in that place than anywhere else. After all, that's what Jesus did. As the parent, full of forgiveness, stood with outstretched arms waiting for the child's return, so Jesus, pleading "forgive them," stretched out his arms and embraced a cross because he loves us.

It wasn't until I was in college that I learned what the word prodigal means—"extravagant, profuse in giving, lavish." The younger son was prodigal in a wasteful way. But in another way, the parent (and our parent in heaven whom this one represents) is also prodigal—giving extravagantly and, in a sense, giving too much. Out of love for us sinners, this Parent gives his child.

The story of the prodigal child, and the selfish sibling, and the Parent who loved them both: as disciples, we are asked to become part of the story. And, if we really have ears to hear the Good News, we will change the world.

Zorba

Then Jesus made the disciples get into the boat and precede him to the other side, while he dismissed the crowds. After doing so, he went up on the mountain by himself to pray. When it was evening he was there alone. Meanwhile, the boat, already a few miles offshore, was being tossed about by the waves, for the wind was against it. During the fourth watch of the night, he came toward them, walking on the sea. When the disciples saw him walking on the sea they were terrified. "It is a ghost," they said, and they cried out in fear. At once [Jesus] spoke to

them, "Take courage, it is I; do not be afraid."
Peter said to him in reply, "Lord, if it is you, command me to come to you on the water." He said,
"Come." Peter got out of the boat and began to
walk on the water toward Jesus. But when he
saw how [strong] the wind was, he became
frightened; and beginning to sink, he cried out,
"Lord, save me." Immediately Jesus stretched
out his hand and caught him, and said to him,
"O you of little faith, why did you doubt?"
(Mt 14:22-31).

Often, our personal life story is greatly influenced and
shaped by other stories—even stories we never expected to
affect us as disciples. But, in a way, that makes a lot of
sense. After all, God calls strangers and misfits to the inner circle of "specially chosen ones." So why can't this God
use all kinds of unexpected stories to bring people into discipleship, to challenge faith, and to show what can be done
by those who believe?

I bought a beat up old paperback copy of *Zorba the
Greek*, by Nikos Kazantzakis, for ten cents at a book sale.
It's one of those great novels that, once you start to read it,
you can't put it down.

On the cover it says this is a "fiery novel about a modern pagan." Alexis Zorba is a cantankerous character, a
rebel; yet he's a man who wakens each day brimming with
life. With childlike wonder he looks at things "fresh," like
he's seeing things and experiencing things for the very
first time. He's a bawdy character who drinks too much
and beds too much. He tells stories about his adventures
with his family, with his friends, with his enemies, with
God. He challenges himself and others, and he isn't afraid
to challenge God. He lives life to the full. A pagan? I think
he's a holy man.

He tells this story about his grandfather:

"Ah, Grandad, may God sanctify your bones! My Grandad was a rake too; just like me. And yet the old rascal went to the Holy Sepulcher and became a 'hadji' [that is, someone who has been on a pilgrimage to Jerusalem]. God knows why! When he got back to the village, one of his cronies, a goat thief, who had never done a decent thing in his life, said "Well, my friend, didn't you bring me back a piece of the Holy Cross from the Holy Sepulcher?"

"What do you mean, didn't I bring you any back?" said my cunning old Grandad, "Do you think I'd forget you? Come to my house tonight and bring the priest with you to give his blessing and I'll hand it over to you. Bring a roast sucking pig, too, and some wine, to bring us luck!"

That evening Grandad went home and cut out of the doorpost, which was all worm-eaten, a small piece of wood, poured a drop or two of oil over it and waited. After a time, up comes the fellow in question with the priest, the sucking pig and the wine. The priest brings out his stole and gives the blessing. Grandad performs the ceremony of handing over the precious piece of wood, and then they start devouring the sucking pig. Well, believe me, the fellow bowed and prostrated himself before that little piece of wood, hung it round his neck, and from that day forth was another man altogether. He changed completely. He went up into the mountains, joined the army, and helped to burn Turkish villages. He'd run fearlessly through showers of bullets. Why should he be afraid? He was carrying a piece of the Holy Cross from the Holy Sepulcher—the bullets couldn't hit him!" Zorba burst out laughing.

"The idea is everything," he said. "Have you
faith? Then a splinter from an old door becomes
a sacred relic. Have you no faith? Then the
whole Holy Cross itself becomes an old doorpost
to you."

In the scripture quoted from Matthew, we hear again
another disciple story about our friend Peter, Rocky. I
think Peter is talked about so regularly in the gospels because he's so believable, he's so human. He's got a good
heart and at times he does the greatest things. At other
times he bungles and makes the biggest mistakes. He gets
excited like a little kid and at times seems to have the
greatest faith. But, at other times, his faith literally sinks
into the water.

Jesus says, "How little faith you have! Why did you
doubt?" Yet Jesus, the believer, still had enough faith in
Peter to give him the keys and to say, "You are the corner-
stone. I build my church upon you, Rock."

This Jesus says "Come" to each one of us, to each of us
in a different way. With faith we can bring out the joy and
goodness of those around us. With faith, we can wake each
morning and hear the flowers and stones telling us their
miracles and watch the trees and birds showing us their
splendor; each morning, for the first time . . . again.

With faith, we can make peace in the world.
Where there is sin, we can bring forgiveness.
Where there is brokenness, we can bring healing.
Where there is sorrow, we can bring joy.
With faith, we can make a kingdom.
"Come!"

HOW ARE WE CALLED ?

My grandmother always wore black. At least that's the way I remember her. It was her way of showing the people in her world that she was still in mourning for her husband, a man who had died many years before.

I was always somewhat afraid of my grandmother, yet at the same time I was fascinated by her. My father had great respect for her and I probably picked up some of my reverence for her from him.

She lived downtown in a bad section, a place that got worse when hatred between races flared up during the sixties. But she wasn't afraid. Into her mid-eighties she still walked to church every day. I was glad then that she wore black. I somehow felt that she was less vulnerable and in less danger that way.

I remember her always praying—I used to think that her fingers were crooked and twisted like they were because she had prayed the rosary so often. It amazed me how much the woman prayed; she never tired of it. I was always on my best behavior when I was with her because I did not want her telling God any damaging stories about me.

She was over at our house the evening her son Owen died. He was young but had been sick and in the hospital for a long time, and my grandmother was doing everything she could for him, keeping a constant prayer vigil. The holy candle that had been blessed by the priest was melting away by her side and I was afraid of what would happen if it burned out.

When the call came saying Owen had died my grandmother wailed in pain and screamed for God to answer the question, "Why?" She hollered like I had never seen or heard before. It wasn't that she had lost faith. Rather, she had so much faith that she was able to yell at God. She was allowed. God was so close to her and so much a part of her life that she could do nothing else at that moment but scream a mother's anguish at the death of her son.

I didn't understand it at the time. I was frightened by the way she was putting God on the spot, yet I was also intrigued by her courage.

A few years later, when I was in the ninth grade, my grandmother died. She had been hospitalized for about a month after having fallen, breaking her hip. She couldn't walk to church anymore and she deteriorated quickly. We knew that the end was near and I, in my heart, prayed that God would allow me the privilege of being near her when she died so that I could be close to the grace that must happen when the angels arrive for someone as holy as my grandmother.

But she died during the night, and early in the morning my mother woke us kids to tell us the news. I didn't want it to happen that way, and I didn't want to hear it that way, and I remember rolling over in bed and telling my mother to go away and to leave me alone. I wanted to get my sleep.

That day I walked around with a chip on my shoulder, with no consideration for anyone else; pouting, that things didn't happen the way I wanted them to; sulking, because my feelings were hurt. I had lots of emotions confused inside me but I didn't know how to express them.

That evening I went to my room and sat in the darkness. A tremendous feeling of grief came over me and I began to cry. Soon I was sobbing like a baby and my body clenched because of the overwhelming anger that I felt. I looked out the bedroom window at the black, empty sky. And I yelled at God for taking my grandmother away. I knew that God understood. God didn't punish me for yelling. Instead, God held me close.

In his wonderful book, *The Spirit Master*, John Shea claims that "desire is the beginning of discipleship." His thesis is that discipleship occurs because people have first been fascinated by the Jesus story. Other people and other experiences in our life have fascinated us in such a way so as to attract us to Jesus. The transmission of stories of faith happens from person to person, in ways that may initially seem merely secular . . .

A young girl learns how to be a mother by first being attracted to and then imitating the affection and care given to her newborn baby sister. Only later will she see its connection with the holy—that the birthing of new life is something miraculous, something sacred.

A young boy is fascinated by the religious practice or devotion that his grandmother demonstrates. But only later in life does he himself demonstrate faith, the core of that devotion, as part of his own story.

The Spirit Christ promises to his disciples has a real presence in the shared faith stories of Jesus. That's why

Jesus could tell his followers, "Today, scripture is fulfilled in your hearing."

The spark that initially attracts us to the Jesus story may show itself in momentary encounters or in long-lasting encounters. We have all had both. Momentary encounters are those fascinations that happen in simple, everyday kinds of ways:

—Pete was a midget who lived in my neighborhood; he struggled to get around and was often made fun of by us kids. I only saw him once in a while but he always had a pleasant smile and a nice thing to say to everyone. . . even me!

—I remember one time we got a flat tire. An elderly man pulled over and helped my father fix it. Afterward, my father offered the man some money for his assistance. But he wouldn't take it.

—On a crowded bus one day I gave up my seat to a woman who was carrying two large bags. She had the most expressive face and the saddest eyes I had ever seen. She thanked me and blessed me with her smile as she sat down. I watched her the whole way home. I somehow sensed that she lived a life of much pain and I wished that I could do more for her.

Long-lasting encounters are fascinations that happen in such a significant way that we find ourselves "apprentices" to the people who have had such a profound influence on us. In some people we see a way of living that changes our own way of living. We see in them a way that we want to go because they mirror for us the possibility of what God has generously offered.

Momentary encounters often cause us to pause and to think, but are rarely the reason for us to drastically change our life. But long-lasting encounters effect in us a real conversion, a real turning in the direction that our true self is called to journey. They mark us in a permanent way and radically alter the way we live with others. Beyond that, they give us a direction to God. They point us to the unique bend in the road that has been designated for our holiness.

Just as each disciple is unique, so are the encounters and the stories. Mary wasn't called to be Elizabeth, and I wasn't called to be Peter. Some are called to be single-parent disciples, others are called to ordination. Some are called to be active in community, others are called to be disciples of prayer living in a place all alone.

But each disciple is given the gifts and talents to hear and to become part of the Jesus story in the way that God intends. Scripture is full of both momentary encounters and long-lasting encounters. The particular ones which affect us and draw us to a fascination with Jesus may differ from those which affect others.

For example, the peripheral and fleeting character in Mark's gospel—the Good Friday disciple who runs away—has always fascinated me. As he begins to flee, his garment gets stuck in the bushes and he runs off naked and vulnerable into the darkness. Where did he go? What happened when he showed up at his next destination, naked? Does he come back to Jesus? Is he possibly the young man sitting at the entrance of the tomb dressed in a new white baptismal garment three days later on Easter Sunday?

The story of the beloved disciple has had a long-lasting effect on me: Who was this special disciple who laid his head on Jesus' heart at the Last Supper? He, along with three women, had the courage to stand at the cross of Jesus and watch him die. Three days later he outran Peter to the place where they had taken Jesus' body; he poked his head inside the tomb and saw the emptiness that filled his heart with belief. And, at the end of John's telling, Jesus says about this disciple, "If it is my will that he remain until I come again, so be it!" This statement of Jesus sparked rumors that this ideal disciple would not die. Maybe it was Jesus' intention that a discipleship that was "ideal" would remain until he came again in glory.

The stories that affect me may be of no great consequence to someone else. Likewise, I may not as yet have allowed the significant Jesus stories of someone else's life to be heard in my life in a real way. It's probably safe to say, though, that all of the Jesus stories, all of the encounters (whether momentary or long-lasting), have the capacity to transmit faith and to influence us as disciples.

Overall, what they clearly do is indicate that the disciple must take the stance of a listener. If we are to hear the gentle voice of God calling us to discipleship, we must listen to the stories of Jesus, we must listen to the people and encounters that astonish and fascinate us, and we must listen to the way that we are story to others.

When I was young I had no clear understanding about the goodness that my grandmother's life was having on my faith development. I only knew of my fascination and love for her. In retrospect, I see how my life and my faith have been shaped by her example. And I see more clearly the importance and influence of all those fascination encounters that I for too long had only taken for granted.

So now, with disciples' eyes, I look back at those encounters and make them real again through story. In the process they become fine-tuned. And if I am lucky, the music in my telling will be heard by other ears, by other disciples who are seeking a song.

So, too, I now comb the stories of Jesus in scripture, reacquainting myself with past fascinations, seeking the encounters I missed before, and coming to see through it all a God who calls us disciples.

Speaking Up

God put Abraham to the test. He called to him, "Abraham!" "Ready!" he replied. Then God said: "Take your son Isaac, your only one, whom you love, and go to the land of Moriah. There you shall offer him up as a holocaust on a height that I will point out to you."

When they came to the place of which God had told him, Abraham built an altar there and arranged the wood on it . . . . Then he reached out and took the knife to slaughter his son. But the LORD's messenger called to him from heaven, "Abraham, Abraham!" "Yes, Lord," he answered. "Do not lay your hand on the boy," said the messenger . . . . "I know now how devoted you are to God, since you did not withhold from me your own beloved son" (Gn 22:1-2,9,10-12).

Jesus took Peter, James and John and led them up a high mountain apart by themselves. And he was transfigured before them, and his clothes became dazzlingly white, such as no fuller on earth could bleach them . . . . Then a cloud came, casting a shadow over them; and from the cloud came a voice, "This is my beloved Son. Listen to him."

As they were coming down from the mountain, he charged them not to relate what they had seen to anyone, except when the Son of Man had risen from the dead (Mk 9:2-3,7,9).

Wouldn't it be nice if God spoke to us more directly? I mean, once in a while, it would be really nice if we could hear a clear, audible voice so that we would know what to do. Peter, James and John were lucky. God did speak to them that way. Jesus had taken them up a mountain. When they got to the top everything became dazzlingly white. Jesus was transfigured before their eyes. Metamorphosis—his appearance was completely changed and they recognized who he truly was. "This is my beloved son; listen to him." And what was it that Jesus said, what were they to listen to? "Don't tell anyone about this," he said, "until I've been raised from the dead." In effect, he told them, "I am going to die."

God also spoke in a clear audible voice to Abraham. Abraham was an old man, an Old Testament disciple. His wife was an old woman. She was a disciple too. They had always wanted children but they had none. But God spoke to them and said, "You are going to have a child." Sarah received the news like any old woman would: She laughed. But they did have a child. So they named their little boy Laughter, Isaac. And now their lives were complete.

So, just when the story has a happy ending, God speaks to Abraham again and tells him to take Isaac, his only son, whom he dearly loves, take him up a mountain and kill him. It must have taken great faith for Abraham to follow this command.

I seriously doubt if I could muster such faith. But God does speak to us. God speaks to all disciples. And often

God speaks in a clear, audible voice. The reason we may not hear it is because we are not listening, or, if we are listening, we may doubt that it is the voice of God. It's difficult for me, as a disciple, to relate to spectacular God stories like the ones we hear about Abraham or the one we hear about Peter, James and John. God may have spoken to those guys in incredible ways, in very unique events, but it's not the kind of experience I have in my everyday life. Unlike Abraham, God has never asked me to take someone I love dearly, a child no less, and kill that child. And it's been quite a while since Jesus invited me up a mountain where he was transfigured before my eyes. But I have to admit that God has, usually in indirect ways, pointed to his Son, his beloved, the one whom he allowed to be killed, and God has said, "Listen to him." Maybe that's the key.

To really listen to Jesus in our daily living, perhaps we need to allow him to be transfigured before our eyes: to allow his whole appearance to be changed before us. Maybe we need to allow our image of Jesus to be transfigured: to get him off the mountain, out of angelic white clothes and without the piercing eyes; perhaps we need to see him in our own home, in the members of our family, in our friends, and even in those we don't like.

I don't know about you, but the God I know isn't big on showing me tremendous displays of power or impressing me with incredible miraculous feats. The God of my experience is subtle, and yet there's been something very profound in that subtle interaction with God. That's why I continue to believe. That's why I tell the story.

Each day I will try to look at people differently. I will remember that each person is a member of the body of Christ and that each person is on this earth literally dying for God. I will hear the voice of God pointing to them, pointing to you, and saying, "These are my beloved."And through my interaction with you, I will try to listen to him.

Stormy Weather

As evening drew on, Jesus said to his disciples, "Let us cross over to the other side." Leaving the crowd, they took him away in the boat just as he was. And other boats were with him. A violent squall came up and the waves were breaking over the boat, so that it was already filling up. Jesus was in the stern, asleep on a cushion. They woke him and said to him, "Teacher, do you not care that we are perishing?" He woke up, rebuked the wind, and said to the sea: "Quiet! Be still!" The wind ceased and there was a great calm. Then he asked them, "Why are you terrified? Do you not yet have faith?" They were filled with a great awe and said to one another, "Who then is this whom even the wind and sea obey?" (Mk 4:35-41).

It is true that the Lord has called me—the problem is, he called collect! He reversed the charges, and I'm not always sure if I'm willing to pay!

Even a peripheral look at some newsworthy events will indicate that we live in a world that is torn and full of violence: hostages being held by people who are full of hate; terrorists blindly attacking innocent victims; children being taught to fight other children in the name of religion, in places like Northern Ireland and Israel, and even some places much closer to home.

We live in a storm of confusion, hurt, pain and violence. And it often seems that our options in dealing with the storm are limited. Many times we ignore what's happening in the present because it's too messy or difficult.

We focus on the "good old days" and live in another world. Or we may recognize the storm and feel called as disciples to do something to make this a better world. But because there's so much to do, because it's so overwhelming, we often find ourselves procrastinating:

"I know it's important for me to really get involved in the life of my community . . . I'll get to it one of these days."

"I know I should be more available to spend quality time with my family and friends . . . I'll get to it one of these days."

"I know I should be concerned about the lack of peace and justice in the world . . .
. . . one of these days."

But we know that the past is gone, the future is uncertain. All we have is today, the present.

The disciples knew the experience of being tossed about in a storm, of being afraid and lacking in faith. So what did they do? They called out to the Lord. And the Lord calmed the storm.

It is fitting that Mark has the disciples say, "Who can this be that the wind and the sea *obey* him?" The verb "obey" is in the present tense, and that means to tell us something about the Lord's activity today.

The life of Jesus is not just an historical event, not just something that happened a long time ago. He is with us today, with us in the boat so that we may safely sail through the stormy sea.

It's a tough world and there is a lot of pain. Yet our faith demands that we call out for the Lord to calm our storms. Then our focus in the present will be a witness to others. It's hard to be a witness of goodness, a disciple of joy, in a world that knows so much pain. But if we try, what a difference we can make!

There is a story you may have heard about two men who shared a room in a nursing home. Both were bedridden. One man occupied the bed next to a window and the other man was across the room in a bed next to the door. Because this man could not see out the window, he asked his roommate to tell him about the happenings in the outside world. So every day, the window side man gave his friend a report. He told him about the postman who made his rounds, wearing raincoats and boots in rainy weather and short sleeves on sunny days. He told him about the lovers who passed the window every day about noon. He described how they first held hands then embraced and then parted. He even spoke about the glances they would give each other showing how much they longed for one another's presence once again. And truly, the door-side man lived for these reports.

One day, however, the man in the bed next to the window died, so another man was wheeled into the room to take his place. The man next to the door introduced himself and then asked his new roommate if he would tell him about the goings on outside the window. "Sure," said the man next to the window. "Only I don't know how I can. There is nothing outside but a brick wall."

It is amazing what a difference "story" can make in our living together. The stories of shared goodness that are offered between people who really care about one another can bring hope, and purpose, and a renewed sense of self. They can have a tremendous impact on the way we understand reality and the way we create meaning from our experiences. It's true, there is an awful lot of pain in the world. But the story of Good News allows us to turn a situation that is dreary and bleak into one that is exciting and vibrant.

The next time you're watching television, turn on the news station. The report, in many ways, will be bleak. There's so much hurt, both outside and inside. But we can weather the storm.

Indeed, Jesus can calm the storm if we call on him. Don't be afraid . . . even if, at first, he seems to be asleep. Call on him. Call collect if you want, reverse the charges. And he will answer with his own Good News.

Epiphany

When Jesus was born in Bethlehem of Judea in the days of King Herod, behold, magi from the east arrived in Jerusalem saying, "Where is the newborn king of the Jews? We saw his star at its rising and have come to do him homage" (Mt 2:1-2).

The world is charged with the grandeur of God . . . Oh, morning, at the brown brink eastward, springs— Because the Holy Ghost over the bent world

broods with warm breast and with ah!
brightwings.

Gerard Manley Hopkins

Discipleship can be described as a personal attachment to Jesus the Christ. This unique attachment shapes the entire life of the one who is called as a disciple. The call is to a supremely personal union, one marked by the initiative of Jesus, and one that is rooted, not in some philosophy or doctrine or teaching, but in Jesus himself. Those who are called do not always seem to possess any orthodox qualifications for membership into his radical band, for the One who often opposed traditionalism, encourages us to be comfortable with our calling despite the fact that we may find ourselves acting in ways that are countercultural.

Discipleship is the fulfillment of our destiny. Often, it is not the thing we seek or the dream we are after. Our society encourages us to be hedonists, to promote and involve ourselves in endeavors that yield instant personal gratification. But people who live that way are not happy. Ironically, when people of the "me generation" begin to acknowledge a dissatisfaction with their own agenda, then the time is right for them to hear the disturbing voice of our surprising God, a voice which calls disciples to live, to see and to seek in a new way. It is a voice much different from the way we thought God sounded. And the better we listen, the more clearly we hear that voice. We even find that, through our hearing, *we* begin to sound different too.

In Flannery O'Connor's short story called "The Turkey," an 11-year-old boy named Ruller is out playing one day when he spots a wild turkey. The bird has been shot; it can't fly, but it can run. Ruller begins to think what a hero he would be if he could catch it and bring it home as a prize for the family. "Wouldn't everyone be so impressed?" he muses.

So Ruller tears after the turkey and he sees himself "edging nearer with his arms rigid and his fingers ready to clutch." He keeps his eye directly on the bird as he runs through field, thicket and hedges. He gets scratched and his shirt gets ripped, but even when he has to get on his hands and knees to get under the fence, he keeps his eye on the turkey. In fact, he's so focused on "the catch" that he runs smack into a tree as the turkey scrambles off into the woods to cover, lost for sure.

Ruller is angry now. All that running for nothing. Why would God go around sticking things in your face and making you chase them all afternoon? He begins to say dirty words and to conjure up bad thoughts figuring he's a bad person so, why not?

When he finally gets up to go home he walks into the woods to see the turkey lying there dead. He can't believe it! Maybe God *was* on his side. After all, God showed him the turkey.

With the bird perched comfortably over his shoulder, he heads for home, the long way through town, so everyone can admire his amazing catch.

The townspeople are impressed. The men whistle at the bird, the women gather close to have a look, and a group of other boys follows behind. Ruller is so proud he could burst and he now figures God must be wonderful so he wants to do something for God. He has a dime in his pocket and he decides to pray that a beggar will happen along so he can show his generosity.

"Lord, send me a beggar. Please, one right now!" he prays. And no sooner had he prayed but there she turned the corner and he felt almost like he had when he ran into the tree. "Here!" he gives her the dime and he's full of a new feeling—like being happy and embarrassed at the same time.

Now, at the edge of town, the boys who had been following him ask to see the turkey. Ruller begins to tell them the hunter's tale in full, heroic detail. But before he can react, the boys have grabbed the turkey and run off, leaving Ruller to stand there alone, empty handed. Now noticing that it's dark, Ruller begins to run home.

"He ran faster and faster, and as he turned up the road to his house, his heart was running as fast as his legs and he was certain that Something Awful was tearing behind him with its arms rigid and its fingers ready to clutch."

I'm afraid that a lot of people only understand Epiphany like Ruller: God shows himself in the prize catch that we decide is important; God reveals herself in the thing, or lifestyle, or whatever that we decide we want, what we are after. God is to be avoided. You don't seek out God. God is that Something Awful that's ready to get us; ready to catch us being bad. Watch Jimmy Swaggart and the TV prophets of gloom: "You need to be SAVED because the spirit of evil is rampant in this age!"

And we in turn become the selfish "something awful" that's ready to clutch what we want, what we're after. Only on the occasions when things go well do we figure, "Well, maybe God ain't so bad after all."

Matthew's gospel story about the birth of Jesus is a switch. These odd ball magi from the east actively seek out a God who is invisible. Like Ruller, focused on that turkey to the exclusion of everything else, these foreigners focus on the star that will show them God manifested. But unlike Ruller, they didn't create a picture of what God's goodness and greatness should be. In fact, the King they seek shows himself as a child in the least likely place. An incredible picture: disciples adoring a little babe at the foot of an animal feeder.

Salvation is not because we are so bad.

Salvation is because we are so loved.

God is not Something Awful that's ready to catch us.

God is Something Good that wants to break into our world; Something Incredible that wants to break out of our hearts.

God is not out to catch us.

We should be out to catch God.

Epiphany. . .

to catch a glimpse of God!

Walking and Waving

As Jesus passed by the Sea of Galilee, he saw Simon and his brother Andrew casting their nets into the sea; they were fishermen. Jesus said to them, "Come after me, and I will make you fishers of men." Then they abandoned their nets and followed him. He walked along a little farther and saw James, the son of Zebedee, and his brother John. They too were in a boat mending their nets. Then he called them. So they left their father Zebedee in the boat along with the hired men and followed him (Mk 1:16-20).

It's amazing how God calls us. The other day, I was heading for an appointment, running late, thinking about a thousand things, and frustrated that there isn't enough time in the day. As I zipped down the road, God spoke to me. It wasn't as if the clouds opened up or some tremendous voice came from the heavens. Rather, it was a little man with a white beard dressed in a brown habit. It was my friend, Brother Isidore.

Brother Isidore is a Capuchin Friar who has become quite a celebrity in my area. Newspapers have written about him, television crews have filmed him, and people all around are always seeking him out. Yet he's not your typical celebrity. Brother Isidore walks a lot—from the Franciscan Friary, up the main road, through the town of Claymont, and on up into Pennsylvania. He walks about 12 miles every day. But he's not renowned because he walks. He's renowned because he waves. To everyone he sees, he waves.

He's a very simple man, a good and holy man, and he has told me that he believes that God wants him to do this, to wave to people and, maybe, bring them a smile. And it works. He's been in this area for less than a year, but already so many people look forward to waving to him each day.

It may seem to be only by chance that he sees any person in particular on any given day. But the origins of his travels, and the reason why he does what he does, is very deliberate. It's as if he was meant to be there and to wave to each person exactly when and where he does. I'm convinced that it was planned for him to be there for me the other day.

From the first chapter of Mark's gospel, we have a story about Jesus calling disciples. He was walking along and waving to people, saying, "Come follow me." It may seem that it was only by chance that Jesus chose those he did, but God's calling is not by chance. It's very precise. The call itself reveals something to us about God. That's why when we feel we are given something to do, we can't ignore it. We aren't able to rest until we act on it. When the disciples heard Jesus calling, something of God was revealed to them. The call also meant a challenge, a challenge to respond to that call through service. That's the difficult part. It's not enough to accept the fact that God has chosen us, or even that God considers us a special part of the plan. The hard part is the price we know it's going to cost us, that we have to give of ourselves in order to answer God's call.

As Simon, Andrew, James and John were to learn, . . . discipleship is not just being with or following after the Lord. Rather, discipleship is a commitment to become like the Lord. Therefore, the disciples called that day in Galilee, as well as those he continues to summon to himself from every part of the world, are to become not merely members but effective architects of the kingdom (Patricia Sanchez in *Celebration*).

Disciples are to be makers of peace in the world and doers of justice to all people.

What Brother Isidore is called to do is to walk along smiling and waving to people. And that's a wonderful thing. But that's not what I'm called to do. That may not be what you are called to do either. But each of us is called. Each of us must listen to the voice of God speaking uniquely to us, we must see God revealed in our gifts and talents, and we must act, building up the kingdom.

WHAT DOES DISCIPLESHIP ENTAIL?

If you remain in me, and my words remain in you,
ask for whatever you want and it will be done for
you. By this is my Father glorified, that you bear
much fruit and become my disciples (Jn 15:7-8).

Getting ready to go away, Jesus made the time to be
with his disciples, to hug them and to tell them what they
needed to do. They were told to carry his story to others,
and thereby bear much fruit.

He described for them what the situation would be like
after he was gone and before he returned. The Christian
community would celebrate in joyful fellowship with the
risen Lord and the Spirit of life, but Jesus also predicted disciples in conflict with a hostile world. There would be ultimate triumph, of course, because the disciples had a victori-
ous God who had pitched a tent in their midst. As he was
going away, Jesus prepared them for their own journey.

So today when we look at our discipleship to see what
it entails, we see journey, a journey that is not always the
shortest distance between two points. Our vocation as disciples often changes as we change in life. We are sometimes called from one place to another. And so we must

ask, "Where are the places to which we are called?" Is it literally a change in location? Is it a change in view? Is it a change in lifestyle?

In the melancholy of her music, Judy Collins tells us about the places in her life that have changed. In "Both Sides Now" she sings,

> I've looked at clouds from both sides now,
> from up and down
> and still somehow
> it's clouds' illusions I recall,
> I really don't know clouds
> at all.

Sometimes, we don't have the vision to see clearly the movement in life that is taking place. Indeed, we may not even be aware that movement has happened, till one morning, wide-eyed, we look around and say, "How did I get here?"

Sometimes the things we thought were stable are passing, and what was considered security is often illusion. And when we look back, it's the vague unknowing that best describes our journey.

But we believe that there is a knowing God in charge, a map-reader who directs us through ways unknown, a God of patience who takes us to both sides of the clouds and shows us their goodness. We may not understand what makes them hang in the sky but it's hard to miss their beauty. And once we've seen their beauty we can't help but tell others about it.

The responsibility of discipleship entails a faithfulness to the Good Story that we've been given to share. To be a disciple is to make other disciples. The line that divides where following ends and leading begins is often transparent and the veil that drapes the two is very thin.

But we live in an exciting time for disciples. Perhaps it is due in part to the fact that communication allows us to see everything so vividly, and so instantly. Cameras take us to the battlefields and show us people being murdered. There's no place for us to hide our eyes. More than any other time, we are very clearly aware of how hostile the world is. But our encouragement lies in knowing that Jesus promises his disciples triumph against that hostile world. And perhaps because there is so much pain and hatred, hearts are ripe for the harvest. People are seeking the Good News that will bring them meaning beyond the madness.

It's an exciting time too in that the people of the "me generation" have lost faith with the empty promises of hedonism and have begun to return en masse to the more basic and simple life ways. People are living better, eating better, and taking better care of themselves. There has been a return to virtue and people are seeking ways to stretch beyond the cynicism that so many wars have induced. People once again are looking for a hero, and the surge of popularity and profound influence caused by such disciples as Dorothy Day, Thomas Merton and Oscar Romero tell us that the Jesus story is alive and vibrant.

In church, too, there has been a significant shift. The hierarchy no longer issues those black and white "no fish on Friday" rules for living. Today, there is more freedom, a freedom that demands more responsibility. The bishops have birthed letters of a pastoral nature on such issues as peace, the economy, and minorities. They present to us the stark reality. We in turn must wrestle with those issues and then decide where our place is in them, what we are called to do.

The laity today is actively involved more than ever before in the ministry of the church. There has been a resurgence of community life, and from the grass-roots level a new incredible voice has emerged, a voice of faith that is leading the church into a new era. Some people are extremely concerned about the decline in the number of ordained disciples and they pray for an "increase in vocations." But many people of faith recognize that we all have a vocation, and they hear the rustling of the Spirit's activity in the present state of affairs. They believe that the God of destiny, who once entrusted the kingdom to a rocky-hearted fisherman, has confident assurance when placing the life of the Christian church in the un-oiled hands of lay leadership.

Finally, when considering what discipleship entails, we can't overlook what is known as the "paradox of discipleship." Jesus told us (was it a warning or an affirmation?) that, "You will be sorrowful, but your sorrow will turn into joy." This "sorrowful joy" is the paradox of discipleship.

The God of contradictions shows us that discipleship entails paradox . . . the first shall be last; the lowly shall be raised high; the meek shall inherit the earth. Jesus himself lived the greatest paradox and has promised the same for us: To live we have to die; to save your life, you must lose it!

Disciples accept the paradox because disciples have experienced sorrowful joy. The world is painful. To ignore the bombs and the killings and the hatreds and the hungry and the children dying and the adults hiding would be insanity. We must identify with the suffering if we are going to make a change. And yet it's in making change that sorrow comes to know joy.

When we embrace the cross we feel its beauty and we remember that Jesus was lifted high on a cross and became triumphant. He gave us the example of dying that we might have life. So there is laughter in our pain and joy in our tears.

—Dorothy Day was often ridiculed because she had a child out of wedlock, a child society named "illegitimate." But her life in Christ mocked the rules of society and made legitimate all of the goodness that she nurtured.

—Thomas Merton was a hermit who took a vow of silence. But the Jesus story would not be kept quiet. From a lonely cabin in the hills of Kentucky came one of the loudest voices for justice and peace.

—Oscar Romero was a priest and a bishop. But even his place as presider at liturgy could not protect him from a bullet that was aimed at Christ. Now, this holy person has a special place in the kingdom of eternal life.

———————

All disciples live the paradox of sorrowful joy. During my years of seminary formation, no one prayed for me as much as my Uncle Jim. No one wanted to see me ordained as much as he did. He was a wonderful man who suffered a lot in his life, but I remember him best, laughing. During the last five years of his dying he fought a monster called cancer. We prayed and fought, hoping that he would live to see my ordination. But it didn't happen. He died.

The day of my first Mass of thanksgiving was tremendously joyful. But I also felt an incredible hurt as I thought of my Uncle Jim. In all honesty, though, I was able to tell the people gathered at that celebration that I had no doubt whatsoever that my Uncle Jim was celebrating with us.

I'm not a hero. I've never done anything great for the

people of God. But I believe that all of our stories count. I believe that when God looks down from heaven and sees us trying to follow Jesus, God smiles.

So I keep on trying to live my life as a disciple—to tell my story of Jesus, and to listen to yours.

Time for a Change

There was a wedding in Cana in Galilee, and the mother of Jesus was there. Jesus and his disciples were also invited to the wedding. When the wine ran short, the mother of Jesus said to him, "They have no wine." [And] Jesus said to her, "Woman, how does your concern affect me? My hour has not yet come." His mother said to the servants, "Do whatever he tells you." Now there were six stone water jars there for Jewish ceremonial washings, each holding twenty to thirty gallons. Jesus told them, "Fill the jars with water." So they filled them to the brim. Then he told them, "Draw some out now and take it to the headwaiter." So they took it. And when the headwaiter tasted the water that had become wine, without knowing where it came from (although the servers who had drawn the wine knew), the headwaiter called the bridegroom and said to him, "Everyone serves good wine first, and then when people have drunk freely, an inferior one; but you have kept the good wine until now." Jesus did this first as the beginning of his signs in Cana in Galilee and so revealed

his glory, and his disciples began to believe in
him (Jn 2:1-11).

The place was Montgomery, Alabama. The year
1955. Mrs. Rosa Parks, a Black woman, was arrested because she refused to give up her seat on a bus to a white
man. Nearby, the new young minister at the Dexter Avenue
Baptist church heard about the woman's story and he recognized a crisis. By definition, a crisis means a turning
point. When one acts in the time of crisis things can turn
for the better or they can turn for the worse. So, crisis has
the capacity for either opportunity or failure. To not act at
the time of crisis always implies failure.

Well, this young minister decided to act. He knew that
it was going to be hard to change the unjust situation that
allowed segregation to continue. But he was a disciple and
his Christianity forced him to try. He joined others in or-
ganizing a boycott of the buses. He was arrested but he
never gave up. In fact, many more joined with him and
within months the Supreme Court ruled that segregation
on buses was unconstitutional.

For the next 12 years of his life, Martin Luther King
Jr. continued to face the crisis and to face it as a Christian,
with the principles of peace and love and justice.

It seems that the purpose of Christ's coming into the
world was to bring about a crisis—a turning point, a decision between light and dark, between truth and falsehood,
between life and death.

There was a wedding feast at Cana. Traditionally, this
story has been used as the source for explaining the sacrament of marriage. But the sign, the miracle that Christ
performed at Cana has nothing to do with marriage. I
have heard it said that since the miracle was changing wa-

ter into wine maybe Jesus was instituting the sacrament of wine-making! Well, that's not it.

But maybe Jesus was instituting the sacrament of change. This Jesus came into our world to change the old into the new. He came to change sinners into lovers; to change hardened hearts into wellsprings of forgiveness; to change apathy into fire and zeal; to change a cross from a curse into a symbol of adoration; to change you and to change me into disciples, peacemakers, martyrs.

By his example so must we live. Martin Luther King tried and because of it he was killed. But he did make a difference. He did bring about some change. But there's still so much more that we have to change.

Martin Luther King spent four years of his life in Chester, Pennsylvania, just a few miles from where I am. And today, ironically, just a few miles on the other side of Chester in southwest Philadelphia there are neighborhoods that won't let in Black people. We must change that.

Each year in January, around the time that we honor Martin Luther King, we also see the anniversary of the legalization of abortion on demand in this country. Since 1973, there have been over 18 million abortions. And that violence continues each day. We must change that.

Throughout the world, terrorism, apartheid, discrimination, and other self-hatreds tell us that this world which God created is an awful, violent place. We must change that.

We must not sit back and ignore. We must face the crisis and choose to make a difference in our own back yards and in the world.

If we don't, who will?

Loving
Like a Mother

Jesus said to his disciples:
"As the Father loves me, so I also love you. Remain in my love. If you keep my commandments, you will remain in my love, just as I have kept my Father's commandments and remain in his love.
   "I have told you this so that my joy might be in you and your joy might be complete. This is my commandment: love one another as I love you. No one has greater love than this, to lay down one's life for one's friends . . . . I have called you friends, because I have told you everything I have heard from my Father. It was not you who chose me, but I who chose you and appointed you to go and bear fruit . . . ." (Jn 15:9-16).

After watching several new scouts at their first attempt at outdoor cooking, the new scoutmaster decided he should intercede. Everything was in disarray, the food was turning out terribly and the young boys seemed rather upset. Finally, the scoutmaster asked, "How are you doing? Have you forgotten any essential equipment?" "Yes, I have," answered one of the scouts. "Oh really, what did you forget?" And the little boy answered, "My mother!"

Mothers are indispensable. Theirs is a job of incredible responsibility—24 hours a day! Mothers must run a taxi service. They must be doctor and nurse. Being a mother means cleaning and cooking and cleaning again and again and again.

To be a mother means trying to ease the pain of a little one who wasn't picked when sides were chosen for the ball game. It means sitting up all hours of the night because your toddler has a high fever or because your teenager decided not to come home. It is a life of many demands and too much pain.

But it is also a life that has its own unique joys and happiness: the joy that comes from sharing a secret—when your little one cups a hand around her mouth and your ear so that no one else in the world will hear the good news, the special message, that binds you in a private covenant, a privileged friendship . . . the happiness that comes with all the many gifts you are given—a lopsided cardboard heart on Valentine's Day; some freshly picked buttercups on your birthday; a hug, a kiss, an "I love you" on that dreary day when you aren't feeling too well.

And only a mother knows the joy of that very special gift: birthing a child. A mother's love is like God's love. A mother's love brings new life into the world.

God's love was revealed in our midst this way: God sent God's only child to the world that we might have life through the love of that child. The child that came to the world transfigured the world. All life was changed because of that child.

Jesus challenged the way things were done and the way people were loved. He didn't ask, he commanded that we love all people. By his own example, by living with the rejected, by loving those who were outcasts, he showed us how we, as disciples, are to love. His way of loving bridges the gap between all divisions. His way of living makes us all members of one body, one family. We are Easter disciples with a resurrected faith and Jesus wants to share with us his great joy: "That my joy might be in you and your joy might be complete."

But how does one share in joy—by reading about it? by

being told about it? No. We share in joy by being a part of it, by being part of the experience. Any parents who have seen their child give a flawless rendition of the Gettysburg Address to the school assembly can tell you what joy is. By being there, supporting and cheering for the kids—being part of the experience—that's joy.

Likewise Jesus, raised from the dead, has come back to his disciples to share with them and with us, the good news that God does not abandon us. God has kept the promise, broken the chains of death and now offers us the gift of peace, a mother's peace.

To share in this joy, to experience this gift of peace is not merely an invitation: "It was not you who chose me, but I who chose you." Think about that. Despite what we may think about how we got here, the fact is, it really wasn't our choice—God has chosen each and every one of us, in a special way. Like a mother who lovingly holds her child, God holds and loves each one of us.

How we respond to that love is our choice. How do we act on it? There's so much wrong, so much hurt and pain in the world. What can one person do?

I was recently reading about a group that is working for the canonization of Dorothy Day. Dorothy Day was one of the founders of the Catholic Worker Movement in New York City. Founded during the Depression, the movement started with a small newspaper that fought for social justice and peace and tried to combat the terrible poverty, physical and spiritual, that existed at that time.

Dorothy Day was once asked, "How, in the beginning, with such extreme poverty and so many obstacles around you, were you able to continue?" She explained, "It was all loaves and fishes. Each charitable act we did, each kindness, each good thing, were all loaves and fishes. No matter how small, we brought it before the Lord and believed that he would multiply those loaves and fishes and make a miracle."

And make a miracle he did. The group found ways to feed and clothe and shelter the poor—first a few, then a few hundred; then thousands. The group went on to found farms and houses of hospitality in New York, Los Angeles, Boston, Washington, and in other cities around the country.

We too must allow God to really direct our lives. We must become part of the experience, no longer spectators, but disciples involved in making this a better place. We too must bring loaves and fishes before the Lord and believe that God will make a miracle. We too must remember that we are chosen and if the kingdom is going to flourish, it depends on the courage and faith and motherly love that begins with you and me.

To Dwell in a House of Parables

You, son of man, I have appointed watchman for the house of Israel; when you hear me say anything, you shall warn them for me. If I tell the wicked man that he shall surely die, and you do not speak out to dissuade the wicked man from his way, he [the wicked man] shall die for his guilt, but I will hold you responsible for his death. But if you warn the wicked man, trying to turn him from his way, and he refuses to turn from his way, he shall die for his guilt, but you shall save yourself (Ez 33:7-9).

"No one has greater love than this, to lay down one's life for one's friends . . . I no longer call you slaves . . . I have called you friends" (Jn 15:13,15).

There is no doubt that the most difficult virtue of discipleship is to suffer. The way of Jesus leads to the way of the cross. This is not an ambiguous point. Scripture and our tradition make it clear that disciples are committing themselves to suffering when they follow the Galilean. Yet, the greatest suffering is bearable somehow when viewed through his embrace; the most excruciating pain is welcomed when we know it will bring us closer to him. Even though the road is topsy-turvy and the story of our simple stroll becomes the incredible journey of parable, we know we will make it. In the final reckoning, there is always comfort and peace for the disciple.

We live in a world that's full of "me" . . . madness, calling itself reason. The language we speak and the story we live is so full of the first person singular that we never find others in our conversation. All alone on an island, stranded by the limits of our words, we see ships passing by but we don't know how to signal for help.

To be saved, we must go down to the water's edge. We must leave the false security of the island's center, the place that "seems" the safest. We must go to the limit of the land. Maybe there we will be heard. We must reach out and touch other persons if we are going to be pulled on board. But people are afraid to touch.

A man comes to church and wonders why he can't find God. He sits in a place alone all by himself so that he can "concentrate." He closes his eyes tight and prays really hard. He prays and waits and waits . . . nothing. In his heart, he figures this must be a joke. But fear doesn't allow him to admit it. So he puts his faith nowhere, in nothing. Ironically, God can be found in doubt. If only the man would speak from his heart the truth that answers questions.

Amazingly, God can be seen in the spaces between people, in the place that hangs between you and me. You don't see God with eyes tightly shut for concentration. You see God in the daily pull between people, in the mistakes and miracles that happen when people care enough to love and to be loved. But people are afraid of love. The news is full of stories about AIDS. Why? For two reasons, I think. One, because we're afraid of things we can't control. And two, AIDS gives us something that seems to be black and white. It's easy to judge when things are black and white.

The other night the television news reported a survey on the question: Would you work next to someone who has AIDS? Thirty-five percent of those questioned said "No," because they just don't know enough about this "thing." Ten percent said "Not sure." And 55 percent said "Yes" because, as one woman put it, "I'm not going to have sex or do drugs in the workplace, so I'm O.K."

The reason the story isn't really edifying, despite numbers that are skewed in a positive direction, is that the question was all wrong. You can't be saved from the middle of the island. You've got to be on the fringe. Questions about "me" when I'm standing on safe ground are meaningless.

There was a man named Jesus who was a "parabler": He told parables that challenged people's worlds. "Love your enemy," he said. "Do good to those who hate you." He lived parables that subverted the way things were; he told his disciples, "Take up a cross. Stretch out your arms, touching others, and you will die. But in dying, you will live."

He walked along the beach, which was at the water's edge. The people on their islands hated him and they told him to die. So he did. But he parabled in death. He confounded their expectations. He didn't die the way a prophet was supposed to . . . in glory, pomp, and exalted circumstances. No, when the time came for heaven to meet earth, he died a most shameful death. They looked up at him and jeered. Their judgement was black and white. They knew this was the greatest folly.

About mid-afternoon, the sky darkened. The island people watched in awe, as there, hanging on a cross, a young man died of AIDS.

A better survey might be done in which people are asked to put themselves on the edge, a survey that asks people about living, not death. The question: If you could switch places with someone with AIDS, and thereby give someone else life . . . would you? People are afraid of life.

Three days later, he rose again,
a Parable!

Cooked Carrots

If I preach the gospel, this is no reason for me to boast, for an obligation has been imposed on me, and woe to me if I do not preach it! If I do so willingly, I have a recompense, but if unwillingly, then I have been entrusted with a stewardship.

What then is my recompense? That, when I
preach, I offer the gospel free of charge so as to
make full use of my right in the gospel
(1 Cor 9:16-18).

St. Paul is a wonderful example of what a disciple
should be. He shows us how he unconditionally accepted
the authority of Jesus, not just inwardly through faith,
but also outwardly through obedience. The relationship
exhibited is much more profound than what is typically
expected between pupil and teacher. Jesus commands and
his disciples obey. They obey because they believe that Jesus is much greater than a master, they believe that he is
the Messiah. They obey because only he can direct each
disciple's unique life to the fullness and joy that it may at-
tain. To do other than what he calls us to do would be just
plain crazy.

Growing up and learning one's place in life is always a
lot of fun. Well, sometimes it's a lot of fun. Well, I guess it
can be pretty awful.

Dinner time was always the craziest time at our house.
In that small kitchen we would gather around the table.
There were eight of us—my mother and father, my five
brothers and sisters, and *me*! Guess which one was the
troublemaker? (Well, somebody had to do it!)

The biggest problem, obviously, was about food! I
hated liver, and no matter how many ways my mother
would try to disguise it, it was still liver and I hated it. But
my greatest dislike was vegetables. Kids go through a period of life when they literally can't stand vegetables.
Their bodies will reject the awful stuff. But parents don't
understand that.

I remember one dinner when I wound up with a plate
of meat loaf, mashed potatoes and cooked carrots. Well,

the meat loaf and potatoes were fine, but I wasn't about to touch those carrots. I ate only what I wanted to eat, although occasionally my mother would break her conversation with my father long enough to look my way, point a finger and say, "Eat your carrots!" Yuck!

Well, as the meat loaf and potatoes dwindled, the carrots became more prominent, they seemed to grow, and by the end I was left with this mountain of ugly, cooked carrots sitting on my plate. My mother was not pleased. She said, "Eat your carrots!", but this time it was said in *that* voice, the one that means she's not kidding around. And what made things worse, my father now added, "Eat your carrots!" When Dad joins in you know it has now become "an issue" and you know you're in trouble. So I tried a kid tactic. I put on that rudely arrogant look (that only children can do to their parents) and I said, "No, I won't eat them!"

Surprisingly, Dad didn't smack me. I wish he had. If he had hit me then I would have felt justified in screaming and crying and running from the table to my room. *And*, I would have gotten away from the dreaded carrots!

But dads can be pretty smart. He decided that everyone else would leave the table and he would sit there, with me, until the carrots were gone. Dads can sit forever, so I knew if I didn't eat those carrots, I would be staying at that table at least through my high school years. So I ate them. . . those ugly, cold, cooked carrots.

When St. Paul talks to us about his vocation as disciple, he tells us that God put him on this earth for a reason—to preach the gospel. That's the reason for his living. He tells us that he had a choice—if he doesn't preach it, he's ruined. If he does it unwillingly, he nonetheless has the responsibility. If he does it willingly, he has his reward. God has given him something to do, and by hook or by crook, he's got to do it, whether he's always happy about it or not. What God expects of him is unique, just as each of our vocations as disciples is unique.

Each of us is called to a special place, a special ministry, a special activity, whether it be in our family, in our parish, or in our community. Is there a group of kids that's waiting for you to come and teach them religion? Is there a congregation that's waiting for you to lector to them or to be a cantor with them? Is there a social or community need that's waiting for you to come and make a difference?

The carrots are waiting to be eaten. The carrots are good for us. And the God who expects something of us, knows what talents we've been given; this God believes in us and knows what's good for us.

Ironically, at my age, I've grown to like carrots very much!

Co-Disciples for the Kingdom

Jesus went out to the Mount of Olives. But early in the morning he arrived again in the temple area, and all the people started coming to him, and he sat down and taught them. Then the scribes and Pharisees brought a woman who had been caught in adultery, and made her stand there in the middle. They said to him, "Teacher, this woman has been caught in the very act of committing adultery. Now in the law, Moses commanded us to stone such women. So what do you have to say?" They said this to test him, so that they could have some charge to bring against him. Jesus bent down and began to write on the ground with his finger. But when they continued asking him, he straightened up and said to them, "Let the one among you who is without sin be the first to throw a stone at her." Again he bent down and wrote on the ground. And in response, they went away one by one, beginning with the elders. So he was left alone with the woman before him. Then Jesus straightened up and said to her, "Woman, where are they? Has no one condemned you?" She replied, "No one, sir." Then Jesus said, "Neither do I condemn you. Go [and] from now on do not sin anymore" (Jn 8, 1-11).

There's a story about the rabbi who was asked to adjudicate a case. The first man presented his argument and the rabbi, after hearing his evidence said to him, "You are right!" Then the second man presented his argument and the rabbi, after hearing his evidence said to him, "You are right!" At this point, the rabbi's wife turned to her husband and asked, "How can both of these men be right?" The rabbi thought for a moment and then said, "Darling, you are right!"

At times, the gospel that comforts becomes the gospel that challenges. Jesus is not some "goody-two-shoes" who would have us believe that his way is easy. Instead, we see the man whose way is the way of the cross, one who looks to his disciples and asks us to follow. We cannot straddle the fence, wavering in indecision, hoping to be left safely alone in the middle. We must make a gospel choice, and then plunge into its full reality. And despite whatever difficulty it may entail, we must believe that his way is the only way for us to go if we are to come to know and to have true life.

The gospel story about the woman caught in adultery demands that we ask ourselves some questions: "How am I judgmental?" "Do I criticize or condemn others because they are not like me?" "Am I open to people who are different from me?" "Do I forgive others when they do wrong and then do I try to affirm their goodness?" or "Do I gossip about others' wrongdoings and add to their painful predicament?"

As disciples, the story also demands that we ask ourselves more specific questions: "How do I treat women?" "Do I recognize the equal dignity of women and relate to them as co-disciples for the kingdom?" "Do I affirm their unique talents and gifts and personhood?" or "Do I sanction, either by my conduct or my attitudes or my refusal to challenge, the sexism that is so rampant in our culture?"

The Catholic bishops of the United States have begun to address the serious issue of sexism in the first draft of their response to women's concerns, entitled "Partners in the Mystery of Redemption." In a quotation from Pope John Paul II, they remind us of the dignity owed to women: "The church proclaims the dignity of women as women. . . a dignity equal to men's dignity, and revealed as such in the account of creation contained in the word of God."

If we are to follow Jesus, then we must have the courage to break down the walls of prejudice and the barriers of ignorance that exist all around us. The gospel refuses to be good news "only for men," or "only for whites," or only for those who fit into *my* narrow categories. We must be willing to challenge our childhood, those times and places and people in our personal history who taught us to be selective and judgmental and narrow. We need the freedom, as individuals and as church, to be able to say that we've been wrong.

I would like to share a poem with you, a modern gospel story written by a man named W. Dow Edgerton. It touches me in a special way because it shows me something of myself and how, as a child, I learned to discriminate and judge others. Maybe there's something of all of us in it. Definitely, there's something of Jesus in it. It's entitled, "Ring-Worm Boy."

"Jesus stretched out his hand and touched him . . ."

He was older than my five or six, and lived on the edge of our neighborhood. We saw him first from a distance. He looked to us like he came from the moon or someplace stranger. He was tall and slender with long supple arms. His head was shaved clean. Over it he wore a kind of cap made of the same stuff as my mother's stockings. He seemed pale compared to us, perhaps because of that naked head, or perhaps he was kept indoors. Who knows? In his face, his eyes looked much too large.

We all stood silent, wondering what this was. Then someone said, "ring-worm, he's got ring-worm." I didn't know that word. Most of us didn't. It could have meant anything—but just the sound was menacing enough: ring-worm, ring-worm. It smacked of the dark and things that live there, the sort of creatures lurking just out of sight in storm drains, who gobbled up rolling money and toys and where we wanted to play but were sternly warned not to. It was said that certain brave boys had climbed down and come back to tell of it. Maybe this moon-child was one. The storm drain did this to him and left him bleached and hairless, like a sailor swallowed by a whale. Someone began to yell, "the Ring-Worm Boy!" And we all began to yell, "the Ring-Worm Boy!" And we all ran away. Always we watched for him. Always we ran. Always we shouted the alarm. Always. Never was there a dare to touch him, never was there a dare to go near, never among us the nerve. We might turn over the rock where the black widows lived, but never did we turn toward him. He was more dangerous to us than spiders.

The Ring-Worm boy had a friend, a girl. We were afraid of her, as well, for surely some of his power had rubbed off on her. Why she was unafraid we didn't think to ask. Still I can see them, the two of them, after we had run away once. At a safe distance I turned and looked: there they stood together on the sidewalk, he with his arms dangling sadly, like a willow, she reaching out to pat his thin shoulder, saying words I couldn't hear.

I shade my eyes sometimes now, and look toward the light to see who might be there. Sometimes it is those two, ringed brightly, their outlines soft in the shining air. She stretches out her hand; she reaches past the fear. Their heads incline, a word is said. Oh a word . . . a word . . . she says a word.

A word I cannot hear.

—Theology Today

Jesus, the maker of disciples, takes a stand. He certainly does not cower in the middle, trying to please all sides. It is obvious that he does not consider a sexual sin to be an end-of-the-world catastrophe. Obviously, too, he does not consider only the woman to be at fault. He straightens up and speaks for truth, defends the woman against such biased judgment and in the process he slaps those petty, insecure men with their own attack and makes them face the power of forgiveness.

Overwhelmed and made inferior by their own sinfulness, they slip away one by one. Finally, it is Jesus alone with the woman that no one could now condemn. Nor does he. He turns to her, not as judge, but as savior. In his gaze, she realizes how important and how very significant she is by virtue of the fact that she is a human person, created in the image and love of God.

As disciples of the Lord, as women and men who follow the example of Jesus, let us hope that others will feel that same realization because of our gaze. In our living together, let others be affirmed in dignity and worth by the way we look at them as Christ.

HOW DO WE DO DISCIPLESHIP?

The Sufi tell a story of great import for the Christian disciple:

> Past the seeker on the prayer rug came the crippled and the beggar and the beaten. And seeing them, the holy one went down into deep prayer and cried,
> "Great God, how is it that a loving creator can see such things and yet do nothing about them?"
> And out of the long, long silence, God said,
> "I did do something about them. I made you."

If we are to do what disciples do, we must remember and deeply involve ourselves with others. Discipleship is not just for myself. It must be generative, it must give life.

At times, we are called to give life in a unitive way:
- —coming together with a special person to be a witness of married love in a divorced world;
- —coming together as a community of believers, to be a witness of shared story in a world that only speaks a language of individualism.

99

At times, we are called to give life in a procreative way:
- —to accept the responsibility of bringing children into the world and growing with them in faith;
- —to use our gifts and talents as a creative force for peace in a world that thinks that real force is nuclear.

All must generate life.

Our membership is with the body of Christ. We are disciples in community. We are not loners, struggling to make a difference in an uphill climb by ourselves. We are part of a group that has a collective life. We have a responsibility to community, and at the same time, we are nurtured by community.

Our lives are often seen as counter-cultural. When the world says "me," we say "us." We embrace the paradox—we forgive our enemies, we do good to those who have wronged us, we die so that we might have life.

It is not by anything of ourselves that we are able to be disciples. We have been commissioned by a very clever God, a God who has gifted us with an abundance of talents and beauty that enables us to do ministry. It is the responsibility of each disciple to nurture the unique talents and reveal the beauty that has been bestowed on us. We must be patient with gifts and always remember to be careful when handling the delicate glories of God.

There's a wonderful story in the book *Zorba the Greek* that reminds us of the care that must be given to treasures. It goes like this . . .

I remember one morning when I discovered a cocoon in the bark of a tree, just as the butterfly was making a hole in its case and preparing to come out. I waited a while, but it was too long appearing and I was impatient. I bent over it and breathed on it to warm it. I warmed it as quickly as I could and the miracle began to happen before my eyes, faster than life. The case opened, the butterfly started slowly crawling out and I shall never forget my horror when I saw how its wings were folded back and crumpled; the wretched butterfly tried with its whole trembling body to unfold them.

Bending over it, I tried to help it with my breath. In vain. It needed to be hatched out patiently and the unfolding of the wings should be a gradual process in the sun. Now it was too late. My breath had forced the butterfly to appear, all crumpled, before its time. It struggled desperately and, a few seconds later, died in the palm of my hand.

That little body is, I do believe, the greatest weight I have on my conscience. For I realize today that it is a mortal sin to violate what we have been given.

Each of us is given all that it takes to be a disciple, to be holy. We find it awkward to think about our holiness— *me* called to be holy, *you* called to be holy. Yet that's what it's all about. Our God longs for us. In the same way, God wants us to long for and wait for God. That longing and waiting is the basic "stuff" of holiness.

Whenever we try to hurry the process or change where we are, we miss the gentle directions that God provides. To be a disciple, I am not called to pray like Peter; to be a disciple, we're not called to live like John the Baptist or Saul of Tarsus. God is pleased with the way God has made each of us; and to be pleasing to God, to be holy, we must simply *be*, people who long for the Lord with the attitudes of basic goodness. It's only with that stance and only in that "breath" that the wings of the kingdom will unfold.

God's design is marvelous. Let it unfold in its natural goodness. Accept your discipleship in the midst of that goodness. Don't rush it. Don't expect any more of yourself than God does. In the same way, don't expect any less of yourself than God does.

Before leaving his disciples, Jesus prayed for them; he also prayed for all future believers, for all disciples who would come to believe because of his story shared through time. And Jesus promised help for his disciples; he promised the Spirit of holiness and truth, the Paraclete who will speak the story through us, so that the world may believe and the Father may be glorified.

Jesus, the Word, came into the world to share his story with us. Now, as disciples, we must continue to share the story with others. We must recognize how we are deeply a part of the story and share that good news.

In his book, *Homiletic*, David Buttrick has a wonderful statement about story and amnesiacs. He reminds us that, "The problem for amnesiacs is not that they have forgotten their names, but that they have misplaced their stories and, as consequence, their identities. It helps little to hand an amnesiac a label—'Your name is Susan Smith'—when the real need is a recovery of narrative identity. So, incidentally, if the church has lost track of identity, titles such as 'people of God' or 'body of Christ' may not help; what is wanted is a rehabilitation of story. Words may name the world, but narrative consciousness tells us who we are and where we are in the world. Story confers identity."

Let us not forget who we are. Without the story, we wander aimlessly like people with amnesia. We can say words, but we have no real idea of who we are and what our purpose is. With the story, we know who we are, we know why our life has meaning, and we know the One who has sent us.

As disciples, we come together in story, and our unique threads are woven into a magnificent tapestry. Full of color and life, this tapestry is the handiwork which allows us to understand

our identity: Christian disciple

our placement: the vestibule of the kingdom
  and

the Weaver: a God of story.

Wrapped in the tapestry of our salvation,

let us be

the good news of Jesus Christ!

God's Candid Camera

Jesus said to his disciples: "Do not be afraid any longer, little flock, for your Father is pleased to give you the kingdom. Sell your belongings and give alms. Provide money bags for yourselves that do not wear out, an inexhaustible treasure in heaven that no thief can reach nor moth destroy. For where your treasure is, there also will your heart be.

"Gird your loins and light your lamps and be like servants who await their master's return from a wedding, ready to open immediately when he comes and knocks .... You must also be prepared, for at an hour you do not ex-

pect, the Son of Man will come"
(Lk 12:35-36,40).

"When you least expect it,
you're elected,
you're the star today!
Smile!
You're on Candid Camera!"

Some are probably too young, but many of us vividly remember the TV show *Candid Camera*. Allen Funt and his crew set up strange situations and then, through a hidden camera, they would watch people in the act of "being themselves."

One of the real classics of the show was the time they came to Delaware and set up a crew at the Delaware-Pennsylvania border. They had blocked all traffic coming in from Pennsylvania to Delaware with a sign that read:

DELAWARE IS CLOSED TODAY!

Some people were furious, some were confused, and some just figured, "Well, I guess we'll just come and visit some other day when Delaware *is* open!"

When you do not expect it . . .

In this story from Luke's gospel, Jesus tells his disciples, "Be prepared, for at an hour you do not expect, the Son of Man will come." A warning. It has a threatening, ominous sound to it. You better be careful what you do, because Jesus is watching!

But is that really the God we know, hiding behind corners trying to catch us doing something wrong?

No, I don't think so.

"Do not be afraid any longer, little flock. Your Father is pleased to give you the kingdom." Jesus does tell us to watch, to be ready. But the same Jesus tells us the kingdom is in our midst. Maybe that's what he wants us to be ready for—those special moments when the kingdom is ushered in and our own preoccupations fade away—when we pull ourselves away from television long enough to see the sky and the trees and all creation, when we stop focusing on all the little things that we don't like about ourselves and suddenly see what a special gift we are. And those times, when you least expect, a kid looks up at us with that scrunched-up face and just smiles . . . and we know that God has smiled upon us.

I think up in heaven God has lots of great pictures of us spread all over a big coffee table—pictures that God took with a candid camera. Pictures of stars. Pictures of us at our best when we were really giving or loving or receiving the gift of God's grace. Extraordinary pictures like the ones we have in our mind's eye:

—the picture I have of Mom, when I was so little and she was singing in the kitchen, so beautiful;

—or the one I have of Kathy when, to my surprise, she said, "Yes!" she'd go to the prom with me;

—or the one of that congregation, the community of disciples, the first time I stood up at the ambo, so afraid, and looked out and all their faces said "Welcome!"

The kingdom is in our midst!
When you least expect it
you're elected
you're the star today.
Smile!
You're on God's candid camera!

It Cannot Be That Way With You

Then James and John, the sons of Zebedee, came to Jesus and said to him, "Teacher, we want you to do for us whatever we ask of you." He replied, "What is it you wish [me] to do for you?" They answered him, "Grant that in your glory we may sit one at your right and the other at your left" (Mk 10:35-37).

The ancient Pueblo Indians are extinct. They simply don't exist anymore. But in a way they still have a lot to tell us. Archeologists and cultural anthropologists have discovered some very striking things about the Pueblo Indians. Most significant is that in their language the Pueblos had no word or synonyms for "competition." Theirs was a culture that did not know the meaning of that word. Hence, their life too was devoid of competition.

In lieu of competition they used cooperation. They worked together peaceably, helping one another, and living in harmony. Unfortunately, neighboring tribes began to attack the Pueblos and, since fighting is part of the competitive mentality (something that the Pueblos did not possess) they did not fight back.

A competitive mentality is engrained in the American culture. It's so much a part of who we are and what we do, that we assume it is always a good thing. Competition, however, is not simply, "I want to win," "I want to succeed." Built into the notion is the flip side, the side we rarely talk about: "I want him to lose," "I want them to fail." We may not articulate it in such brutal terms, but that is part and parcel of what it means to be competitive. And Jesus has something very clear and very direct to say about it.

James and John were competing against the others. They wanted the top positions next to Jesus when he came into his glory. And Jesus said, "No. Your wanting something like that is wrong. You should be thinking of others most of all and yourselves least of all."

Ironically, they had asked for one of them to be at his right and the other at his left when Jesus came into his glory. But that distinction was given to two criminals: one hanging on a tree to his left and the other to his right.

As part of a Christian community, is our focus competition or cooperation? The world and our church are changing so quickly. Today, with the decline in the numbers of priests and sisters, the church is calling lay people to take charge, to continue the work of Christ in a new collaborative way. It is wonderful to see so many gifted women and men who are listening to the Spirit and making such a tremendous contribution to the body of Christ. But there's always more to be done.

That's why the church needs even more disciples giving of their time and their talents. Look around the community. Think about some of the needs that are yet to be fulfilled. Think about your gifts and talents. We are called to use them. And when we do, when we work together, when we cooperate, there is no limit to the good that can be accomplished.

The Pueblo Indians lived a life of cooperation. And because of it, they were killed. When you're dead, you're dead. And that's the end of it. Or is it?

Jesus refused to compete or to allow his disciples to compete. He lived a life of selfless giving. And because of it, he was killed. When you're dead, you're dead. And that's the end of Jesus. Or is it?

107

Philadelphia

Come now, you rich, weep and wail over your impending miseries. Your wealth has rotted away, your clothes have become moth-eaten, your gold and silver have corroded, and that corrosion will be a testimony against you . . . . The cries of the harvesters have reached the ears of the Lord of hosts. You have lived on earth in luxury and pleasure; you have fattened your hearts for the day of slaughter. You have condemned; you have even murdered the righteous one (Jas 5:1-6).

I went to Philadelphia one afternoon this week . . . decided to do South Street. Philadelphia is a great store-front window. It grabs your attention: vendors, incredible buildings, wonderful stores. South Street is a dazzling neon sign in that store-front window. It's warm and inviting with its many specialty shops, curiosities and avant-garde strollers.

I was window shopping; enjoying the afternoon, enjoying being anonymous. Up ahead, I could see a guy asking passers-by for something. He was young, about 24. He was muscular with long, unkempt brown hair. He was wearing jeans and no shirt. His body was well-tanned, a tan that comes, not from lying on the beach, but from standing outside and being exposed to the sun: deep and dark brown on the shoulders and arms, and gradually lighter down the chest and stomach. This type of tan doesn't have the glow that comes from prepping oneself with expensive creams and oils that smell like coconut. It is flat and always seems a little dirty.

I assumed he was asking people for a cigarette. He looked like the cigarette type.

One by one the people he bothered shook their heads "No" shrugged their shoulders, or just ignored him. All walked on.

I was closing in and thought to myself that since I hadn't smoked in over two months, I really wouldn't be lying when I told him that I don't have any cigarettes. Somehow, I felt good about that.

It was my turn.

"Hey buddy, can you spare some change?"

His question threw me. I wasn't expecting that at all. My reaction was to shake my head "No" and walk on. I felt him walking behind me:

"F— man! This isn't me. I don't want to do this. I'm a mason. But I can't get a job."

There was both anger and apology in his voice. And I wasn't sure whom he was angry at: me? . . . or the world? Or whom he was apologizing to?

After he spoke to me I experienced "one of those moments": a split second (that seems forever) when you have to make a decision. You know if you don't decide right away, you lose the opportunity. At those moments, the mind has a remarkable capacity for image-making. I say "image-making" because it really isn't "thinking." Thinking is a more deliberate process that involves time and consideration. Here, an image flashes in the mind: an image so full and vivid that you feel you really know something. Perhaps it is the stuff of which insight is made.

At any rate, I suppose the image that flashed in my mind could be best described as "Savior." I envisioned myself stopping, turning to this outcast, and with a look that says, "I care," changing his whole world. After all, I have lots of connections! I could get him a job, get him back on track. I'm a professional Christian! It's my life to reach out to those who have been disregarded, to those who are hurting and angry. At the very least, I could give him what money I had in my pocket—about $58. Not really salvation, but to someone who was only asking for "some change," imagine the impact of a total stranger kindly stopping, assuring him with a look that indicates empathy, not condescension, then handing over money and, without having spoken a word, quietly walking away.

The image had flashed in my mind. Because it was only a flash I didn't have time to think about it. I could only react.

His words, full of anger and apology, still rang in my ears . . . . It was time to act.

I tightened my fists around the money in my pants pocket (as if I were protecting something sacred). I lowered my head and felt a frown forming on my face, and quickly, quietly, I walked away.

Philadelphia . . . the city of brotherly love.

The Body of Christ

Jesus said:

> "I am the living bread that came down from heaven; whoever eats this bread will live forever; and the bread that I will give is my flesh for the life of the world.
>
> "Just as the living Father sent me and I have life because of the Father, so also the one who

feeds on me will have life because of me"
(Jn 6:51,57).

When we were little we didn't see things as "big" as we do now. Our perspective was limited. Our focus was narrow. We saw the world, and everything in it, through our own incomplete vision, our personal understanding. I remember when I was in the second grade. My teacher was Sister Patrick and you can be sure that when St. Patrick's Day rolled around we were going to celebrate it in style. That was fine with me because I was Irish and I figured that was the absolute best way to be.

When the day came, everybody wore something green and Sister had a party for the class. She asked students to come up to the front of the class if they knew an Irish song that they'd be willing to sing. A little girl got up and sang "When Irish Eyes are Smiling" and a boy sang a part of "My Wild Irish Rose" and I was bursting with pride inside because it was now my turn. Not only did I know an Irish song—I knew an Irish song that was written about *my* family name, or so I thought! I now know that the song, from the musical *George M,* is called "Harrigan," but I had heard my father sing it with his own lyrics, and I thought for sure that it was written about us because we had such a famous Irish name.

I can still picture Sister Patrick standing there laughing when I got up and started to sing: C, O, double R, I, G, A, N spells Corrigan! Later, when I told my parents the story, they laughed too, and it was only years later, when I got bigger, that I found out why.

I think when we were in the second grade we also had a really incomplete understanding of Eucharist. "Corpus Christi," the priest said, "The Body of Christ." We received the host on our tongue because it was alright for Jesus to touch us but we dare not touch Jesus. And we'd go back to our pew, kneel down, close our eyes, and be all alone with the Lord—just me and Jesus—nobody else; that was the high point in Mass. We'd be "sanctified" (whatever that meant), a little better than we were before, and that was that!

Now, I think we see things about the Eucharist in a bigger way. And I think we have the disciple John to thank for that. Remember Matthew, Mark and Luke give us the Last Supper story about bread and wine. But John's Last Supper story talks about Jesus washing the apostle's feet, about service. St. John must have been one of those kids who was different—sort of an oddball. He probably wore glasses, studied a lot and won all the spelling bees.

I can imagine one day in class when the teacher did that "pass along game" with the students whereby something is whispered to the first kid, who whispers it to the next kid, and so on, and so on, and by the time it comes around to where it started, it's completely different from how it began. With John's class it probably went something like this:

Mark whispered to Matthew: Jesus loves us so much that he broke bread and poured wine and said, "This is my body, this is my blood. Do this in memory of me."

So Matthew whispered to Luke: Jesus loves us very much so he took some bread and broke it and he took some wine and poured it and he said, "This is my body, this is my blood. Do this in memory of me."

So then Luke whispered to John: Jesus, out of love for all of us, took some bread and wine. He broke the bread and poured the wine and he said, "This is my body, this is my blood. Do this in memory of me."

And now it's Johnny's turn. So John whispers: Jesus loves us so very much that he took an apron and wrapped it around himself and he washed people's feet. He said, "I have given you an example. Do this in memory of me."

We know Eucharist as the food and drink that brings us together at table. But we also know Eucharist as bodies that are broken in a quest for justice, as love that is poured forth to liberate those who are oppressed. When a presider at a liturgy holds up the bread and wine, open your eyes and see not only our sacred food, but also the body of Christ as stretching forth one's arms for others. When you say "Amen," it is a double affirmation. This *is* the body of Christ that you receive, and you *are* the body of Christ to be received. It can't be one without the other.

Back in the second grade, on the feast of Corpus Christi, we used to have a big procession where we'd carry the monstrance all around the church. And that was good.

Today, our "procession" is when you walk out of your house or through those church doors into a world that is starving for the bread of life. To hear the whisper of the kingdom's inbreaking we must be disciples who are willing to whisper to others. So whisper to all the world, or at least to the kid in the next desk, "The body of Christ."
Amen.

Forgive Me

If any one has caused pain, that person has caused it not to me, but in some measure—not to put it too severely—to you all. For such a one this punishment by the majority is enough; so you should rather turn to forgive and comfort that person, or they may be overwhelmed by excessive sorrow. So I beg you to reaffirm your love for that person . . . . Any one whom you forgive, I also forgive. What I have forgiven, if I have forgiven anything, has been for your sake in the presence of Christ (2 Cor 2: 5-8,10 *RSV*).

Disciples of the Lord Jesus should be strangers to the unhealthy guilt that festers within hearts that have either been unable to give or to receive forgiveness. Too many people cannot say the words, "I forgive you". . . possibly because they cannot believe that they, though unworthy, are continually invited by our God to receive the grace of forgiveness.

Jesus, in dying for us, opens his arms and offers an everlasting embrace. In breathing forth the Spirit of holiness, Jesus prayed for our forgiveness. But he remains alone on that cross until we are able and willing to accept the gift. Real forgiveness happens when we allow ourselves to touch and be touched by those outstretched arms. Only in the coming together does an embrace happen between two lovers. Only in accepting forgiveness are we truly capable of forgiving.

Are there wounds that have not been healed?

Are there broken places where we have been that need to be mended?

I remember a childhood pain that happened when I was either 11 or 12. I was probably 12 because I think it was my last summer with a crew cut. I hated crew cuts and after that summer, my father did not make me get my hair cut that way anymore.

I was out on the back street alone, up at the corner. I was playing with my baseball bat, a Louisville Slugger. I was standing by the telephone pole hitting stones up at the street light. I was hoping to break it. I would lob a stone a few feet over my head and as it descended I would swing straight up with my bat. A good hit and I would clang the metal light cover; a bullseye and glass would shatter. I don't know why we kids were always doing such things, but we did enjoy breaking stuff. People are always damaging things. It's just the way of the world, I guess. I never did figure it out. Anyway, somebody always came along within a few days to fix the broken light and give us a new target.

At one point, I finally hit the light bulb, but the stone didn't break it. It just ricocheted into the metal cover and then fell, defeated, into the street.

I was bored with the street light.

It was about mid-morning. I have a clear image of how the sun felt and it was too cool yet to have been later than mid-morning. By noon, the summer sun was always too hot and the humidity was very heavy. Now, it was just right. The sun was bright and everything was still fresh, with a light dew on the grass. As I walked toward our house I spotted a robin hopping on the hill in our back yard. The Daniel Boone in me took over. With what seemed to be great stealth, I crept toward the magnificent game bird. When the bird saw me, it stopped. Surprisingly, as I slowly continued toward it, it did not fly away. My heart began to race as I imagined myself catching it. Later I would explain to Mom all the reasons why she should let me keep it.

For example: "But Mom, this is a full grown bird!"

Many times before, I had brought home captured baby birds of different species which Mom said I couldn't keep because:

"It's just a baby. Leave it alone!" or

115

"It must be sick. Leave it alone!" or
"Everybody knows baby birds carry germs and give
people diseases. It's going to die. Leave it alone!"

You could tell this bird was fully grown because of its
size; it was probably the biggest robin I had ever seen. But
you could also tell because of its magnificent, full red
breast. A young robin always has some black and white
downy feathers mixed in with the red. This robin's puffy
chest was all deep red.

The robin looked straight at me as I stood, very still,
two feet away. It was crouched low to the ground and
pulled its wings slightly apart as if it was going to take
flight or maybe even charge at me. For some reason, I was
afraid it might attack me.

The robin's mouth was half open and I didn't know
what that meant. I've seen people do the same thing with
their mouth when they were afraid. I thought about waving the bat to see what the bird would do but I realized that
would only scare it off. My only chance would be to take a
swing at it. It was a long shot, granted, because birds are
extremely fast. But maybe I could graze it and then, having confused it, I would lunge at the bird and capture it
with my bare hands!

I slowly maneuvered my wooden club into the batter's
position. The bird crouched lower still and its new expres-
sion gave me a sense that I was doing something wrong.
Regardless, I swung down fast and hard.

The juices of a prized home-run hit ran through my
body as the bat smacked the robin on the head and it tum-
bled down the hill. But in that same moment those juices
became the adrenaline of panic as I recognized the dam-
age I had done. The bird lay there gasping for air, its eyes
bulging, blood coming out its beak, and its pointed
tongue jutting in and out. I cautiously went near it. I

knew that the bird could not hurt me now so I went to pick it up. The moment I raised it off the ground the bird's head fell to the side. Its neck broken, I felt the robin die in my hands.

Up until that point, I had never experienced such raw shame and guilt and panic. I looked around, fearing that my mother might have seen me through the kitchen window. She was always in the kitchen. I started to run with the bird, not knowing where I was going, but convinced I had to get away. I ran to a wooded lot, looked around to make sure I wasn't being watched, then tossed the dead bird into some overgrown bushes.

Now, I felt tremendous guilt. Not only had I, completely without reason, brutally killed one of God's most beautiful creatures, now I didn't even have the courage to own up to it or to give it a proper burial. Like the true coward I was, I just tossed it aside. But I could not toss away my shame, or my fear.

I ran home as fast as I could, went to the basement, and in the large basin by the washing machine, washed my hands over and over again. I stayed down in the basement for a long time because I was so afraid.

That day I learned how very much a person can hate himself.

Finally, I went to church, to the cold box of confessions, and I whispered my sin into the hidden darkness. A priest told me words of forgiveness and I felt somewhat better. But I still felt incomplete. I still felt dirty. No matter how many times I washed my hands I still carried with me the death of that bird. For such a long time after the crime, I was still swinging a bat. I was still damaging . . . still breaking.

Then one day, while talking to a friend about broken places, I told the story about the robin. This disciple-friend looked at me straight to my heart and asked, simply, "Why don't you forgive yourself?"

At last, I had heard the right words. I faced myself, the real barrier to my healing, and finally I allowed myself to say the words, "I forgive me."

It was on that day that God showed me a new room in my heart.

Now, all these years later, I know much about the love and forgiveness of God because I have experienced it many times. Only a God who is all forgiving would raise his only child to life after we beat him to death with our bats. Only that God would call as disciples those who would abandon the One that love taught them to follow. Only an all forgiving God would send that child to us again, to offer us peace.

I have been moved to great emotion because of the forgiveness of God. I have sobbed and wept in purgatory, from the depths of my bowels, because of the amazing goodness of God. Indeed, I believe in God as forgiveness. And I know that it is a relational grace. It is something intimate that happens when a damaged heart is touched by love.

Now, each year, with the oncoming signs of spring, I still stop in my tracks when I spot the first robin of the season. And I give thanks to a God who melts away our sinfulness and brings us new life. A voice of love chirps merrily as it tries to draw me near.

As I journey on, marking a new path on the remaining snow, I breathe deeply and smell the sweet breath of God.

DISCIPLESHIP PLACES

Now that very day two of them were going to a village seven miles from Jerusalem called Emmaus, and they were conversing about all the things that had occurred. And it happened that while they were conversing and debating, Jesus himself drew near and walked with them, but their eyes were prevented from recognizing him. He asked them, "What are you discussing as you walk along?" They stopped, looking downcast. One of them, named Cleopas, said to him in reply, "Are you the only visitor to Jerusalem who does not know of the things that have taken place there in these days?" And he replied to them, "What sort of things?" They said to him, "The things that happened to Jesus the Nazarene, who was a prophet mighty in deed and word before God and all the people, how our chief priests and rulers both handed him over to a sentence of death and crucified him. But we were hoping that he would be the one to redeem Israel; and besides all this, it is now the third day since this took place. Some women from our group, however, have astounded us: they were at the tomb early in the morning and did not find his body; they came back and reported that they had seen a vision of angels who announced that he was alive.

> "Then some of those with us went to the tomb and found things just as the women had described, but him they did not see."
>
> And he said to them, "O how foolish you are! How slow of heart to believe all that the prophets spoke! Was it not necessary that the Messiah should suffer these things and enter into his glory?" Then beginning with Moses and all the prophets, he interpreted to them what referred to him in all the scriptures. As they approached the village to which they were going, he gave the impression that he was going on farther. But they urged him, "Stay with us, for it is nearly evening and the day is almost over." So he went in to stay with them. And it happened that, while he was with them at table, he took bread, said the blessing, broke it, and gave it to them. With that their eyes were opened and they recognized him, but he vanished from their sight (Lk 24:13-31).

Emmaus is a wonderful place. When I studied in Israel, I learned that, according to today's calculations, there are at least seven different geographic claims for this ancient destination. That's somehow appropriate. It's better to not be so precise in labeling a place like Emmaus. It's better that we remain open when trying to pinpoint the location of such a frontier town. Emmaus is a lot of places. It is a favorite journey for disciples.

The Emmaus story is about post-resurrection disciples and for us today it's such a great disciple story because it contains so many of the elements that personally ring true in our own experience. It typifies so much of what the discipleship of Jesus is all about. It delineates some of the key features of discipleship. Thus, despite the modern discrepancy over where Emmaus actually is, Emmaus as story becomes a road map for us, guiding us on our way and shaping us as disciples.

Emmaus is journey. Despite its contemporary trendiness, "journey" really is an apt and authentic description of the Christian life. From the womb to the tomb, the human person is in process.

One of the classic metaphors used to describe this "in process" or journey of the Christian disciple is "pilgrimage." From the time of St. Augustine, pilgrimage has been both a figurative description, as well as a literal practice, of disciples. His *City of God* is one person's autobiographical account of humanity's journey to heaven. Helena, in the 4th century, was the first actually to go on a journey to the Holy Land. Today, pilgrimage to holy places— Jerusalem, Mecca, Lourdes, Rome—is a significant part of many people's lives.

But pilgrimage or journey also has a symbolic meaning. Disciples are pilgrims who live *in* the world but are not part *of* the world. Their recognition of the transitory nature of the world and human experience and their own lives can lead to a greater appreciation of the here and now, a thankful posture for the many gifts that we have been given. They come to see and to know that each "place" along the developmental road of life is yet another valuable treasure molding their discipleship.

So Emmaus, as journey, represents one of those places we've traveled to; it's a good place to gather, to be opened, to be fed; and it's a place that we're traveling from, a point of departure as we go off as witnesses to proclaim that we have seen the risen Lord.

Emmaus is about the presence of the Lord.

How often is the Lord walking along with us but we fail to recognize, we fail to hear? The New Testament describes disciples as having the posture of a listener. The formal place of the disciple was not to engage in discussion with Jesus. In fact, discussion with Jesus was started only by his opponents. The disciples of Jesus were always listeners who, on occasion, put questions to Jesus when they did not understand.

But like those two dusty travelers talking about "everything that had happened" yet oblivious to the One who was with them, how often are we just gabbing away, in tune with our own gossip, our own yapping, our own wordiness, but oblivious to the Word?

Matthew Fox summarizes this state of mind in his creation-centered book, *Original Blessing*:

> Left-brain hegemony since the Enlightenment has produced a culture that inundates us in the verbal. Advertisers, newspapers, presidential speeches, paperback books, voluminous libraries, and now word processors are all busy changing the meaning of the word "word" and in a sense cheapening it by the very overuse of words. If we are to regain our own lives, our spiritual roots that nourish us into growth, we must return to the pre-word times of original creation; to the time before the printed word, the radio word, the word processor, the printing press; to a time when there was so much silence about, that words still meant something significant.... The spoken word, the storied word, the word that gave birth.

There is so much before us, yet somehow we fail to see. There is so much goodness that should be burning within our hearts and yet we often fail to really hear and understand. Emmaus reminds us that disciples must listen if we are to hear, disciples must focus if we are to see.

Emmaus is Jesus patiently traveling with us, informing us, revealing to us, making the connections for all our scattered pieces. Jesus shares the word with us, a personal and formative union that consequently impels us to follow. It is he who gives both the form and the content to our relationship with him. But, ultimately, it is in his action, in the relationship, in the breaking and sharing of that loaf, that the miracle happens. As Gandhi reminds us, "God appears to you not in person, but in action." At the Emmaus place, Jesus offers himself. In the breaking of the bread, the disciples remember what Jesus commanded them to do in his memory, their eyes are opened, and they see.

Emmaus is about eyewitness. Witness to Jesus is the task to which disciples are called. Sometimes we see it all at once as was the case with our two Emmaus friends. Suddenly, their eyes were opened to what had been before them, though hidden, all along. At other times, we see things slowly, a dawning sunlight at the beginning of a new story. Most times, the journey is difficult and what we see along the way can be very painful. As we know, committing yourself to discipleship is committing yourself to suffering. But Jesus assures us that there is always comfort for those who die with and for him. What we have seen, the object of our proclamation, does indeed become good news, despite the cross we carry.

I remember one time when I was traveling to Emmaus. It was about three years ago and I was a newly ordained priest. I had gone to visit a patient in the psychiatric unit of a hospital. As I was walking through the unit to his room, a young man came up and asked me if I had some time to talk to him. I told him I would after I had visited the other man. So he waited for me out in the lounge, and after my visit with the other man, I went with this young man to his room.

We sat down facing each other and I could see that he was terrified. He told me that he had wanted to see a priest for a long time, that he wanted to go to confession, but that he was afraid to, afraid that he couldn't be forgiven. He had been praying about it that afternoon when he saw me walk into the unit and he figured maybe God was answering his prayers.

It was very difficult for him to tell me his story. He was 19 years old and he was in the pysch unit because he had tried to kill himself. He was a good looking boy and I wondered why someone like him would try to commit suicide.

He told me that he had always been in trouble, that he had always been in fights with his family. So when he was 15 years old, he ran away from home and went to New York. There, he did drugs and crimes and other awful things that a 15 year old will do when he's lost and hurting and doesn't have anyone to take care of him.

My heart was so full for this young man, and then he told me the hard part. He told me that, about a year before, he found out that he has AIDS. As soon as he said the words, I felt my body become tense. Until that time, I had never actually met anyone with AIDS, and I was immediately afraid. I thought, "Oh my God, we shook hands when I came in here! And now I'm sitting in his chair! And what about the air that I'm breathing in this room?"

Thinking back, I don't know if he saw the fear that was inside me, the selfish panic that stemmed from ignorance. But I pray that he didn't.

He went on to tell me that when he found out he was sick, he didn't know what to do so he went back home to his parents and told his family the story. His father spit at him and told him to leave, to never come back; his mother said he was not her son, and his brother and sisters told him they did not know him.

So he went off and tried to kill himself, and someone found him dying and brought him to the hospital, and here he was in the psych unit. Here was this 19 year old boy, full of the knowledge that he was dying from AIDS, full of the knowledge that nobody loved him, and scared to death that God would condemn him. For whatever reason, God put him with me.

Emmaus can be a very difficult journey. The way of discipleship has a very hard side. And yet a moment in the presence of God, being touched by the power of true sacrament, is so very real and holy, that at those moments, we gladly set aside all our thinking fears and give ourselves over to God.

Healing and forgiveness took place, not only for this young man, but also, maybe more importantly, for me. I needed to be healed of the blindness, the selfishness that allowed me to so easily reject others; I needed to be forgiven for the judgment that I so quickly, even unknowingly, attached to someone with AIDS.

This young boy was now crying and he reached out for me and he held me in his arms as I prayed the formula for absolution. I told him how sorry I was, and I told him about how God loved him, so very, very much. And in that embrace, in that absolution, God reached down, and touched us both.

That was three years ago, and so I remember.

The Christian disciple must thrive in the midst of paradox. The life of the disciple must be one of relinquishing control, of constantly "giving it over" to the One, the absolute and only one, who can and will sustain us. The words of Jesus the prophet are words of one who was rejected.

The people would not hear what he had to say because his words were too challenging to the way they understood their comfortable world.

The memory of Jesus is dangerous because it entails an expectation to follow a drifter; a man who suffered much, was rejected and, ultimately, was murdered as a criminal. And yet, in his memory, we become disciples; we become Christ-like ourselves and our touch has the power to transform the world.

Our brother is dying . . .

our sister is dying . . .

we are all dying.

And, in the midst of such pain, Jesus, who calls disciples, offers us the gift of eternal life.

"Touch, and be healed," the story finishes.

"Touch, and be my healing for the world!"

This final section of the book is about Emmaus places. Reflection on the Emmaus story has taught me about post-resurrection discipleship. As I try to apply some of the things that I have learned to my own journey, I see pieces of Emmaus, parts of the disciple story that have been traveled by me.

I hope others will be able to travel Emmaus in their own story—to hear how the gospel sounds when one considers oneself a disciple, and to encourage others to read their own story in light of discipleship.

Some may find Emmaus a foreign place, or an unfamiliar name in their travels. They may feel that their disciple places are not near Emmaus. Many may feel more comfortable in Bethany or Jerusalem or Galilee or even up an old sycamore tree. But all of us have been offered the grace that allows the stories of these places to touch our own experience. And we find that when we open our hearts and our lives to the holy places of the Jesus story, a new sense of being a Christian disciple occurs. We are filled with a new knowledge and a new awareness because we have been there. In the breaking open of the story, we have seen the Lord. We are privileged to call ourselves disciples of Jesus—a tremendous boast indeed! This discipleship is not the first step with the promise of greater things to come. Rather, it is the fulfillment of our destiny.

As eyewitnesses, we share the story so that others may hear and be touched by the places of our words. In that touch, others may hear their own call, share the story, and continue to proclaim the good news of Jesus Christ.

So I finish with stories . . . Emmaus places, pieces of the journey that have helped to shape me and have helped me to understand my relationship as disciple to Jesus.

I proclaim what I have seen. I share where I have been. And I ask you to story as well.

A Visit to the Beach

[Jesus] entered a village where a woman named Martha welcomed him. She had a sister named Mary [who] sat beside the Lord at his feet listening to him speak. Martha, burdened with much serving, came to him and said, "Lord, do you not care that my sister has left me by myself to do the serving? Tell her to help me." In reply the Lord said to her, "Martha, Martha, you are anxious and worried about many things. There is need of only one thing. Mary has chosen the bet-

ter part and it will not be taken from her"
(Lk 10:38-41).

One of the Emmaus places that I love to go to is on the
Atlantic ocean—Rehoboth Beach, my favorite get-away
spot. As much as I love it, however, "beach" places are also
a little weird. (That's probably why I love it so much!)
Have you ever noticed how people dress at the beach?
Now, you know they only dress that way because they're
away from home. Think about it. How many people do you
know would walk through their own neighborhood wearing a cap that has a styrofoam shark-head attached to the
front of it? Or, how many people do you know would go to
work wearing a tee-shirt that reads, "PARTY NAKED."
(I was thinking about having one printed that reads,
"PRAY NAKED," but I knew that somehow my bishop
would find out about it!)

And the things that people do while they're at the
beach! It still amazes me that one of the busiest activities
on the boardwalk is an adventure called "Wac-a-mole."
You've probably seen it, or done it. People line up to dish
out 50 cents a shot so they can frantically swing away with
a padded mallet at plastic moles as they pop their heads up
out of the holes. Whoever "wacs" the most moles wins a
stuffed animal. It's truly amazing.

One day I was sitting on a bench on the boardwalk directly across from the Wac-a-moles. As I sat there watching for a while, what struck me was all the activity—not
just Wac-a-mole, but also the other games, as well as the
general activity of so many on the boardwalk who seemed
to be looking for what they would do next. All that busy-
ness, all that activity, except for an elderly woman I saw
sitting on the next bench. She wasn't watching the wac-a-
molers; in fact, she was looking out the other way—

toward the ocean. She didn't even seem to notice the noise and activity of all the other people. With a very peaceful and contented look on her face, she seemed somehow removed from it all. At one point, I even found myself looking out over the ocean trying to see what she saw. And I think I know what it was . . .

"Martha, Martha, you are anxious and worried about many things. There is need of only one thing."

How many times have we been Martha, busying ourselves and our lives to the point where we find ourselves frustrated? And when we want to relax, what do we do— plop ourselves in front of a TV which occupies us so that we don't have to think for ourselves. Or, we go on vacation, where, because we're so used to keeping busy, we find that we never really slow down. We just busy ourselves with other details, other activities.

But even at that, every once in a while, the rhythm of the ocean and the pounding waves catch our eye and pull us in. We may not think about the sea's power, or its wonder, or about the God who has given to us so many signatures of created handiwork, but we are caught by it nonetheless. And, in those moments, we know that the world is so much more and so much bigger than all our little details and all the things we do that we think are so indispensable, so important.

One thing only is required. Mary, assuming the status of a male disciple by sitting at the teacher's feet, has chosen the better portion. She's attentive to the word of the Lord . . . and she shall not be deprived of it.

God has given the world, and each one of us, so very much; too often we're too busy to see it.

Someone once said, "I don't know how to love God." And the response came, "So, at least let God love you!"

129

Every once in a while, disciples need to go to the beach, or the mountains, or the woods, or wherever that place is where eyes can be opened and hearts can be filled. There we can really see the many gifts God has given us—our family, our friends, our own wonderful lives!

Let's choose the better portion!

Let the Children Come to Me

And people were bringing children to [Jesus] that he might touch them, but the disciples rebuked them. When Jesus saw this he became indignant and said to them: "Let the children come to me; and do not prevent them, for the kingdom of God belongs to such as these. Amen, I say to you, whoever does not accept the kingdom of God like a child will not enter in." Then he embraced them and blessed them, placing his hands on them (Mk 10:13-16).

Disciples need to keep children's eyes, to see as a child sees, to laugh (giggle) as a child does, to remember that one of the most descriptive verbs associated with God in scripture is "play." Adults too often forget how to play because they "work" so hard.

Annie Dillard walks through the woods, praying to the God of creation by being attentive to all the goodness around her. She has that rare gift of being able to put words together in such a marvelous way that God is made present to us readers or the hearers, even when we're far away from the trees. She shares a wonderful story called "Seeing." It's about a place where disciples need to go more often. Part of the story goes like this:

> When I was six or seven years old, growing up in Pittsburgh, I used to take a precious penny of my own and hide it for someone else to find. It was a curious compulsion; sadly, I've never been seized by it since. For some reason I always "hid" the penny along the same stretch of sidewalk up the street. I would cradle it at the roots of a sycamore, say, or in a hole left by a chipped-off piece of sidewalk. Then I would take a piece of chalk, and, starting at either end of the block, draw huge arrows leading up to the penny from both directions. After I learned to write I labeled the arrows: SURPRISE AHEAD or MONEY THIS WAY. I was greatly excited, during all this arrow-drawing, at the thought of the first lucky passer-by who would receive in this way, regardless of merit, a free gift from the universe. But I never lurked about. I would go straight home and not give the matter another thought, until, some months later, I would be gripped again by the impulse to hide another penny.

I think Jesus came into our world carrying a lot of chalk, and fancy finger paints, and crayons (a box of 64 assorted colors!). Because of the way God likes to color, it's so much easier for childlike disciples to see what God has done on sidewalk-hearts and on construction paper faith. But too many of us, too often, carry around our ball-point pens and our legal-size note pads and floppy disks. Then we wonder why we don't see what's happening, and we hurt because no one sees how wonderful we are.

Trying so hard, we crane our necks and squint at the sun—but it's too bright, and we can't see anything!

Annie Dillard says it best:

It is still the first week in January, and I've got great plans. I've been thinking about seeing. There are lots of things to see, unwrapped gifts and free surprises. The world is fairly studded and strewn with pennies cast broadside from a generous hand. But—and this is the point—who gets excited by a mere penny? If you follow one arrow, if you crouch motionless on a bank to watch a tremulous ripple thrill on the water and are rewarded by the sight of a muskrat kit paddling from its den, will you count that sight a chip of copper only, and go your rueful way? It is dire poverty indeed when a man is so malnourished and fatigued that he won't stoop to pick up a penny. But if you cultivate a healthy poverty and simplicity, so that finding a penny will literally make your day, then, since the world is in fact planted in pennies, you have with your poverty bought a lifetime of days. It is that simple. What you see is what you get.

Disciples, open your eyes and see the pennies! Open your heart and feel the touch of God!

Peace, Bountiful Peace

Jesus said to his disciples: "I have told you this while I was with you. The Advocate, the holy

spirit that the Father will send in my name—
will instruct you in everything and remind you
of all that [I] told you. Peace I leave with you; my
peace I give to you. Not as the world gives do I
give it to you. Do not let your hearts be troubled
or afraid. You have heard me tell you, 'I am going away and I will come back to you.' If you
truly loved me, you would rejoice that I am going
to the Father; for the Father is greater than I.
And now I have told you this before it happens,
so that when it happens you may believe . . . . the
world must know that I love the Father and that
I do just as the Father has commanded me. Get
up, let us go" (Jn 14:25-29,31).

Peace is probably the most wonderful disciple place.
It's the place that Jesus leaves us as a gift so we can find
him and be close to him whenever we are hurting, or
alone, or depressed, or just fed up with everything else.
When we go to this disciple place, we should set markers
of goodness along the way so we will remember the path.
Then, we will be able to return there, time and time
again. The more familiar we are with the road that
brings us there, the more easily we will be able to bring
others there as well. It is definitely a place that must be
shared.

In a delightful movie called *The Trip to Bountiful*,
Geraldine Page stars as Mrs. Watts, an elderly woman
who wants one thing more than anything else in the
world: to return to the little town where she grew up, a
place called Bountiful. She hasn't been there in 20 years
and now she lives in the big city with her hen-pecked son
and her nagging daughter-in-law. They won't take her
back to Bountiful, but Mrs. Watts knows that she will

have peace only if she gets to visit Bountiful one more time before she dies.

So she escapes from her demanding family and, by hook and by crook, and even by begging a ride, she makes it back to Bountiful—back home—and she finds her peace.

At the end of John's gospel we hear the story about Jesus returning home—home to his Father. Knowing that this will distress his friends who don't want to see him leave, Jesus offers them the gift of gifts: his peace!

We talk a lot about the peace of Christ, and in a way it may seem like a contradiction because at the moment the world in which we live doesn't seem so peaceful, what with the horrible acts of terrorism, a maniac ruling Libya, hostages held captive, people oppressed in Africa because God didn't give them another skin color.

So what does peace mean? What is it all about? For a soldier, peace might mean no more war. For a mother, peace might mean sitting quietly in a favorite chair with all the kids in bed—asleep! For someone who is ill peace might mean a period of rest, a time without pain. For a youngster, peace might mean a day at the beach. Each of these is a facet of peace.

The peace which Jesus offers is much greater than all of them. His gift of peace changes the world. And the paradox is: we receive it most fully by giving it away. That doesn't mean that it's our responsibility to resolve all the conflicts between the U.S. and Russia, or to convert all the atheists in the world, or to bring harmony to all the war-torn countries.

But it does mean that we should try to end the conflicts in our own neighborhoods, and be examples of faith to all we meet, and it is our responsibility to be makers of harmony in our own homes.

Is there
—someone who feels loved because you stepped into his or her loneliness?
—someone who was hurting but now can smile because you cared?
—someone who was persecuted but now knows acceptance because you were a friend?
—someone who is working for justice and felt encouragement because of your example?

We can make the world better only by doing what Jesus did: touch it with his gift of peace.

In the movie, *The Trip to Bountiful*, the ending has the son and his wife driving out to the old abandoned house in Bountiful, coming to get the mother to take her back to the city. At this point the nagging daughter-in-law is furious with Mrs. Watts and she rattles off a list of demands that the poor old woman must abide by in the future:

"You will not run around the apartment!"
"You will not sing your Christian hymns!"
"You will not pout!"
"You will answer me when I ask you a question!"
and then she says,
"Now Mother Watts, is there anything you want to say to me?"

The whole audience is now sitting on the edge of their seats, waiting for this sweet old woman to punch that girl in the face! But she surprises us. She just leans forward and kisses her daughter-in-law on the cheek.

She returned home; she found peace—real peace, and she shows it by making peace—by giving peace away.

Receive the peace of Christ!

Be peacemakers in your world!

A Place Called Celibacy

Jesus' disciples said to him, "If that is the case ..., it is better not to marry." He answered, "Not all can accept [this] word, but only those to whom it is granted" (Mt 19:10,11).

I write and include this "disciple place" not only for myself, not only for all the men and women who live as celibate disciples, but also for all the men and women who are called to be disciples, though not celibate. One way is not any better than another.

"Every once in a while I mourn the fact that I will never have children; I have a need to cry, to grieve, for the children I will never know."

A sister whose name I can't remember, a woman affiliated with a religious community, said that to me a long time ago when we were together on a spiritual retreat. Her words went deep inside me, like a huge divining drill seeking water for the thirsty inhabitants above; to the place of power and resource, the place of importance inside me, where I return again and again for meaning. It is a statement that was nurtured in her because she lives a life of chastity, and it has a unique resonance within me because, as a priest, I live a life that is celibate.

Contemporaries in the modern religious world usually think about celibacy only in its positive sense: It's a gift, a unique opportunity caressed by the grace of our (celibate) God that allows one the freedom to be readily available for others, to be free to go wherever and whenever the Spirit leads. In the old days (pre-Vatican II), celibacy was often described as a tremendous sacrifice that one had to endure for the sake of the kingdom. I think it's a little of both—both gift and hardship.

I don't think of God as being very celibate. I think of God as being "in communion with" all of God's wonderful creation. Most people probably would not have a difficulty with that. After all, God is part of all that is good. The problem enters when I make the associations from "communion" to "sexual." (If being sexual isn't communion, I don't know what is!) People don't like to think of God as something sexual. But to me, the God who sent the Son to us, the God who is continually birthing new life, has got to have at least the character of something sexual. Folks naturally bring God into their physically human world by describing God's activities in ways such as: "God's eye (providence) was watching over her," or "God's arm (power) was with him." But if I were to talk about being fed by God's nipple (nurturance), the prudish around me, clutching their narrow and limiting God notions, might run away screaming, "Heresy!"

So, for the sake of the faint-hearted, I will leave God's sexuality out of it and I will restrict myself to the words at hand that deal with celibacy in a more conventional way.

I'm glad that I'm celibate. Now don't get me wrong, I do hurt from time to time because I don't have someone special who is always with me to share all of life's wonderful surprise moments. And it always pulls at my heart to see a young couple with their little one at the mall, or the park, or the zoo. Put me with the Jones family when the children are going through their bedtime routine and I become instant envy. And my loins do ache more often, I would suppose, than the average Joe's.

Celibacy as a call, graced by God, comes complete with all the "stuff" necessary to see the celibate through. That stuff can only be described as certain gifts. Likewise, there are gifts that married/familied people have that enable them to do what they've been given to do, gifts the celibate may not possess.

I recently spent a week's vacation visiting my sister and her family in Nevada. My other sister and her two youngsters were vacationing with us as well. I learned a lot that week. I learned about bottles and diapers and the habits of small humans who use their fingers to eat spaghetti and their feet to blow kisses. I learned about five- and seven-year-old girls who regularly need to have their hair fixed in very specific ways, but who absolutely cannot wear the same piece of clothing twice in one week. I learned about schedules: being able to quietly clean a house while little ones nap, and being able to do the major part of meal preparation during those few rare moments when children aren't underfoot. I learned about patience: Mommies, amazingly, never give up on their girls and boys when they are learning something new; Daddies, exhausted after 12 hours at the office, come alive when their little one wants to play ball. I learned a lot about love.

It is probably what I learned about the incredible responsibility that accompanies family life that assures me that the celibate place where God has taken me is where I most belong. To be called to marriage and to a family is a holy and powerful privilege. But in a world that treats lightly the sacredness of commitment and relationship, marriage and the creation of family cannot be entered into carelessly. It requires devotion, tremendously hard work, and a myriad of life sustaining gifts, gifts that the author of life has not written in my biography.

But for me, celibacy opens the door to a new world, a place that allows me to live and be different. (Despite a cultural paranoia that fears and belittles anyone who is unique, "different" is a marvelous place to be!) One of the real advantages in my difference has to do with the way I focus and make connections. Married folks with families are forced temporally to see things with an eye to the future. It only makes sense. They live for each other—working together, building a home, planning for their retirement. They live for their children—charting a little one's growth with regular height marks on a closet door; encouraging a baby to crawl so that she will one day be ready to stand, and then walk, and then run, and then journey. Married folks have to look ahead.

Celibates, however, don't have to live with this type of future focus. I have the freedom to turn my head over my shoulder and look behind me. That's not to say I live in the past. But I can look back more keenly than others. I have more time to visit with our ancestors, the communion of holy ones who have gone before us, to listen to their stories, to hear their voices, and then to tell others about their abiding love.

Theirs is a world that is sorely neglected. Theirs is an anonymous kindred vainly calling out to their earthly family. The voices are mute to most because ears can't hear. People of the modern world think it's "primitive" to respect and honor the spirits of the dead. They feel there's nothing to be gained by focusing on "what was."

As a priest I have sadly noticed how many people today even want to minimize our relationship to the dead. At the time of someone's death many people only allow themselves a peripheral exposure to the ritual we call funeral. No wake, no mourning, no personal involvement in the ceremonies. Just the basic prayers, bury the dead one, and let's be done with it. I suspect that, in this way, people think they are avoiding pain for themselves and others. But they fail to see that we need rituals of death because we are a people who live and die. Funerals should be a celebration of life and a promise of fidelity to the one who has passed away. We need to mourn because we are a people who love. Only those who have not loved can honestly say they need not mourn.

Perhaps that's something significant about celibacy. I'm mourning for all of us, trying to dignify, by my hearing and telling, all the voices around us, those who have lived before us, those who are not being heard. I mourn and honor and respect and listen to our dead ones until that time when someone else is able to hear. And when that someone else begins to hear, then I can focus anew, listening to another lonely voice, telling again another story of love. And so it goes.

I began this "place" telling about how I mourn for the children I will never have and I finish by telling about the ancestors we have all had. Both are related.

As for the children I will never have, my pain is eased by the generosity with which you share your children with me. (Is this why so many call me "Father"?) They bring to me a beauty and joy and goodness that is like nothing else in the world. You share your children selflessly and I thank you. And the best part of all—I don't have to change their diapers!

As for those who have gone before us, my words here should not be preachy or chastising. Rather, my voice should simply be an encouragement to all of us to try to listen more deliberately and more authentically. There is a goodness, a richness, a holiness that surrounds us, just waiting to be heard. It is as telling as a grandmother's laugh and as personal as a father's "I love you." It is as strong and as real as the journey of those who have walked the earth before us. Indeed, while on this earth, it is the closest we will ever come to hearing the voice of God.

Let those who have ears, hear!

ENDING WORDS

I remember the day it arrived; it was about 40 feet high, about a hundred feet around. It was immense—that amazing, metal water tank!

They lifted it into place with the help of a large crane and they gently sat it down on the east side of St. Bede Hall, right on the spot where it remains, and has become, no doubt, another great landmark on the seminary grounds.

For some reason, they left it empty for a long time. But it didn't take me long to stick my head into the two foot circular opening on its side, into its darkness, into that massive chamber where I shouted "Hello!" and heard for the first time the Echo! whose sound was no less than awesome.

Next, I crawled into the huge canister and inched my way over to its black center; and I began to play with sounds. I whispered, I shouted, I sang. The Echo took my sounds and played them back again and again and again.

Soon there were four of us seminarians in there and we laughed and sang and laughed some more. The acoustics were powerful, the resonance superb. You couldn't see it, but you could feel and hear the Echo, taking our flat notes and making them rich and strong. The Echo amplified and multiplied our four-part, somewhat harmonic rendition of "Alleluia" and made it 16 part, then 64 part, then: the choirs of angels in heaven.

It gave us back a lot, then less and less, till finally it
faded away . . . into silence.
And so I remember.

———————

This book was written about discipleship —
What it means to be a disciple.
How we are called as disciples.
What discipleship entails.
How we do discipleship.
Disciple places along the way.

It is a book about how disciples relate to other disciples; it
is about how story relates to Story. Ultimately, we are all
called to share our stories as part of the Christian Story.

To remember, to repeat, to echo again,
is the story of the children of God and how we have,
through time, lived our lives.

This book is a piece of my story—some of the journey:
the struggle and joy, the movement of life. In a way, this
book is also a piece of our story, and these thoughts, words
and deeds have been recorded in an effort
to remember —
the love of God that has been heard in a Word made
flesh;
to repeat —
the stories that make credible the life we live
together;
and to echo again —
the soft whisper that is heard by "those who have
ears" as the kingdom of God breaks into our world.
Let us continue to hear and to tell . . .
. . . the disciple story.